KL

Collins
Graded Examples
in Certificate
CHEMISTRY

Collins
Graded Examples
in Certificate
CHEMISTRY

W. E. Rosser and D. I. Williams

Collins:
Glasgow and London

Preface

Answering graded, examination-type, structured and objective questions is the accepted way of providing the regular cycle of revision and assessment so important to pupils doing CSE and GCE courses.

Accordingly, this book provides a source of such questions, arranged in sections and topics, and in the teaching sequence found in most schools.

The questions in each section are graded, the easiest being set first. They are sufficient in number, in the authors' experience, to consolidate the learning of each topic in a reasonable time, for example, by providing enough homework for one or two weeks depending on individual progress.

An objective 'test' is provided at the end of each chapter, covering a number of topics. If desired they may be set at monthly intervals during the course.

The chapters correspond to those in COLLINS CONCISE CERTIFICATE CHEMISTRY and the questions were designed with this in mind. Although it would be advantageous for pupils to have both volumes, we believe that this book will prove very useful on its own.

W. E. Rosser and D. I. Williams

W. E. Rosser is Headmaster of Rivington High School, St. Helens;
D. I. Williams is a Senior Lecturer at the City of Liverpool College of Higher Education.

Illustrator   A. J. Steel

© 1979 W. E. Rosser & D. I. Williams
0 00 327742 9
First Impression 1979
Printed in Great Britain by
William Collins Sons & Co Ltd
Glasgow

Contents

SECTION ONE   THE NATURE OF CHEMICALS

SECTION TWO   FACTORS WHICH CONTROL CHEMICAL REACTIONS

SECTION THREE   CHEMICALS AND THE ENVIRONMENT

Instructions for objective tests

Rubric A   Five choices are given in answer to the question of which only **one** choice is correct. Write down the letter which indicates your choice of the best answer.

Rubric B   All the questions relate to a set of given answers—A, B, C, D and E. Write down the letter (or in some cases, the letters) which is (are) the correct answer(s) to each question

Rubric C   Answer each question by writing down **one** of the letters A, B, C or D, as follows:
   A   If only 1, 2 and 3 are correct.
   B   If only 1 and 3 are correct.
   C   If only 2 and 4 are correct.
   D   If only 4 is correct.

Summarised directions for responses to Rubric C			
A	B	C	D
1, 2 and 3	1 and 3	2 and 4	4

Rubric D   Answer each question by writing down **one** of the letters A, B, C, D or E, as follows:
   A   If both the assertion and the reason are true statements and the reason is a correct explanation of the assertion.
   B   If both the assertion and the reason are true statements and the reason is **not** a correct explanation of the assertion.
   C   If the assertion is true but the reason is a false statement.
   D   If the assertion is false but the reason is a true statement.
   E   If both the assertion and the reason are false statements.

Summarised directions for responses to Rubric D			
	assertion	reason	argument
A	true	true	reason **is** a correct explanation
B	true	true	reason **is not** a correct explanation
C	true	false	not applicable
D	false	true	not applicable
E	false	false	not applicable

Abbreviations used

(aq)   —in aqueous solution
bp   —boiling point
°C   —degree Celsius (Centigrade)
(c)   —in the crystalline state
cm^3 —cubic centimetre (1/1000 of litre)
d   —decomposes
dil.   —dilute
dm^3 —cubic decimetre (equal to 1 litre)
e.m.f. —electromotive force
F   —Faraday
(g)   —in the gaseous state
g   —gram
ΔH —heat change (enthalpy change)
J   —Joule
kg   —kilogram
kJ   —kilojoule
(l)   —in the liquid state
M   —molarity (moles per litre)
m^3 —cubic metre
mol   —mole
mp   —melting point
(s)   —in the solid state
s.t.p. —standard temperature and pressure
V   —volt

Atomic weights

aluminium	Al	27	nitrogen	N	14
calcium	Ca	40	oxygen	O	16
carbon	C	12	potassium	K	39
chlorine	Cl	35·5	silver	Ag	108
copper	Cu	64	sodium	Na	23
hydrogen	H	1	sulphur	S	32
iron	Fe	56	zinc	Zn	65
magnesium	Mg	24			

The periodic table

group

period	1	2				transition elements							3	4	5	6	7	0
1	H 1																	He 2
2	Li 3	Be 4											B 5	C 6	N 7	O 8	F 9	Ne 10
3	Na 11	Mg 12											Al 13	Si 14	P 15	S 16	Cl 17	Ar 18
4	K 19	Ca 20	Sc 21	Ti 22	V 23	Cr 24	Mn 25	Fe 26	Co 27	Ni 28	Cu 29	Zn 30	Ga 31	Ge 32	As 33	Se 34	Br 35	Kr 36
5	Rb 37	Sr 38	Y 39	Zr 40	Nb 41	Mo 42	Tc 43	Ru 44	Rh 45	Pd 46	Ag 47	Cd 48	In 49	Sn 50	Sb 51	Te 52	I 53	Xe 54
6	Cs 55	Ba 56	La* 57–71	Hf 72	Ta 73	W 74	Re 75	Os 76	Ir 77	Pt 78	Au 79	Hg 80	Tl 81	Pb 82	Bi 83	Po 84	At 85	Rn 86
7	Fr 87	Ra 88	Ac* 89															

La*—the 14 lanthanide elements
Ac*—the actinide elements

The numbers are atomic numbers of elements.

11

SECTION ONE
THE NATURE OF CHEMICALS

Chapter 1   Physical separation

1.1   Physical separation

1 Draw up a table to classify the following substances as *solids, liquids* or *gases*.

coal, oil, paraffin, ice, water, salt, treacle, glass, tar, mercury, air, butane, iron, baking powder, ice cream, butter

2 Draw up a table to show the *state* of the following substances at ordinary room temperature and at 200°C.

water, lead, butter, iron, mercury, lighter fuel, salt, iodine crystals, sulphur, sand, air

substance	state at room temp.	state at 200°C
e.g. water	liquid	gas

3 Write down the names of simpler substances found in these mixtures.

mixtures	simpler substances
wet sand	
sea water	
rock salt	
air	
lemonade	
lawn fertiliser	

4 Classify the following under the headings *chemically pure substance* or *mixture*.

copper(II) sulphate(VI), lead, petrol, stainless steel, solder, water, absolute alcohol, glass, oxygen, carbon.

5 In each case write out the property which is important in separating the following mixtures. The properties are:

physical form, difference in particle size, difference in boiling point, difference in solubility, difference in density.

mixture	property
oil and water,	
dusty air	
gold 'dirt'	
water and alcohol	
copper(II) sulphate(VI) solution	
dirty water	
copper filings and salt	

6 Each of the properties listed in Q. 5 corresponds to one of the following named techniques. Pair them off.

e.g.	evaporation	—	difference in bp
	fractional distillation	—	
	filtration	—	
	dissolving	—	
	distillation	—	
	decantation	—	
	panning (or centrifuging)	—	
	picking out (sorting)	—	
	settling	—	
	crystallisation	—	

7 Write in the sequence of techniques needed to obtain the underlined substance in a pure form.

mixture	sequence of techniques
e.g. <u>salt</u> and sand	— solution, filtration, evaporation of filtrate, crystallisation
tar and <u>sand</u>	—
aqueous <u>lead(II) nitrate(V)</u>	—
wet <u>acetone</u>	—
suspension of <u>chalk</u> in water	—

1.2 Soluble and insoluble substances

1 Draw up and complete the following table:

14

solution	solute	solvent
aqueous copper(II) sulphate(VI)		
silver(I) nitrate(V) solution		
alcoholic silver(I) nitrate(V)		
dilute sulphuric(VI) acid		
brine		
limewater		
bench ammonia		
tincture of iodine		

2 Use the information given to construct answers to **a**, **b** and **c**.
Substance X is soluble in water but not in alcohol.
Substance Y is soluble in alcohol but not in water.
Substance Z is insoluble in both alcohol and water.
  a How would you obtain pure X and Y from a mixture of both?
  b How would you obtain pure X and Z from a mixture of both?
  c How would you obtain pure Y and Z from a mixture of both?

3 Explain:
  a When a sample of clear well-water was evaporated a white deposit was left.
  b When a clear solution of potassium nitrate(V) was cooled, crystals formed.
  c When the top was taken off a lemonade bottle it fizzed.
  d When tar sticks to a car it can be removed with paraffin.
  e You cannot sink far in the Dead Sea.

4 Five separate beakers contained equal volumes of the same saturated solution. Describe what you would see in the following cases.
  a Water was added.
  b Extra solute was added.
  c The beaker was allowed to stand for a week.
  d The beaker was cooled.
  e Extra solvent was added.

5 How would you test a sample of soil to see if it contained soluble compounds?

1.3 Miscible and immiscible liquids

1 Write down miscible or immiscible opposite mixtures **a** to **c**.
  a mercury and water
  b oil and water
  c paraffin and petrol
  d Which of the above substances would form the bottom layer in the immiscible mixtures?
  e How can oil and water be separated?
  f What would happen if you heated equal volumes of mixture **c** using a fractional distillation apparatus?

15

2 In the fractional distillation apparatus shown there is a mixture of two miscible liquids A and B. A has a bp of 92°C. B has a bp of 56°C.

a What will be the temperature at X as the first drop of B condenses?

b What will be the temperature at Y just after the last drop of B condenses?

c What will be the temperature at X just after the last drop of B condenses?

d Will the temperature at Y be below or above 92°C as the first drop of B condenses?

e Will the temperature at Z be below or above 56°C as the first drop of B condenses?

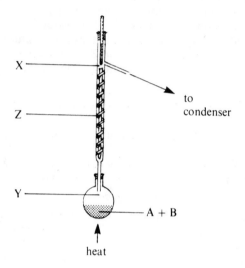

3 Use the following information to suggest how to separate the mixtures.

a mixture of M and N
b mixture of M and P
c mixture of N and P

	bp°C	density	miscibility
M	156	2.20	immiscible
N	184	1.10	miscible
P	42	1.20	miscible

1.4 Sublimation

1 Use the data to decide which of combination XY (ammonium chloride and sodium chloride); YZ (sodium chloride and iodine); and XZ can be separated by sublimation. Write out the procedure for each one that you think is possible.

X (decomposes at 500°C; sublimes at 335°C)

Y (mp 801°C; bp 1413°C)

Z (sublimes 81°C; mp 114°C; bp 184°C)

2 Diagram **a** represents a test-tube of ammonium chloride being heated, **b** represents a test-tube of aluminium foil and bromine. State what is present at X and Y in each of the reactions and explain the changes.

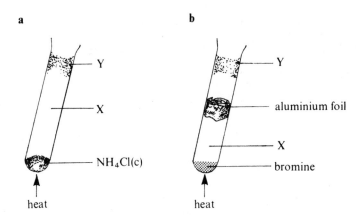

1.5 Chromatography

1 A long strip of filter paper was dipped into purple potassium manganate(VII) solution. Explain these observations.
  a The paper absorbed the liquid.
  b The water was absorbed further than the purple manganate(VII).
  c When the water was so far up the paper it seemed to stop.

2 The following paper chromatogram was obtained.

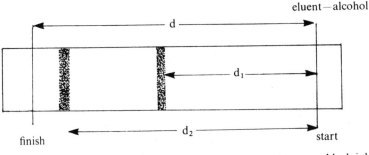

  a How many dyes seem to be present in the black ink?
  b Might there be more? Explain.
  c How can each dye be separately recovered?
  d What is meant by eluent?
  e What is meant by stationary phase?

17

1.6 Criteria of purity

1 Fit the following facts into the information matrix indicated.
  a The mp is 78°C.
  b The %C is always 92·3.
  c When recrystallised from benzene the mp changed.
  d The mp varies between 80–110°C.
  e When recrystallised from benzene the mp remained unchanged.
  f The %C varied from sample to sample.

matrix	mp	% carbon	mp on recrystallisation
naphthalene paraffin wax			

2 Some crystals of a chemical were filtered and then dried in an oven. A mp was determined. It was 113°C. The crystals were washed again by passing more solvent through the filter paper. On drying the mp was found to be 116°C. How do you account for this result?

3 A chemist had two bottles of aniline but he suspected that one liquid was contaminated with impurity.
  How might he find out which one, even if he did not know the bp of aniline? What additional information would he get if he knew the bp?

Objective test 1

Apply Rubric A instructions

1 Which of the following is a solid at 25°C?
  A mp 0°C; bp 100°C   D mp −95°C; bp 69°C
  B mp −40°C; bp 78°C   E mp 3°C; bp 193°C
  C mp 114°C; bp 444°C

2 Which of the following is **not** a chemically pure substance?
  A common salt   D sulphur
  B sodium   E anhydrous copper(II) sulphate(VI)
  C aqueous silver(I) nitrate(V)

3 Which of the following differences makes fractional distillation possible?
  A differences in density   D differences in solubility
  B differences in miscibility E differences in bp
  C differences in mp

4 Which of the following methods would be **best** for purifying alcohol contaminated with a broken mercury-thermometer bulb?

A filtration   D decantation
B centrifuging   E distillation
C chromatography

5 Which is the best sequence of techniques for separating salt and chalk to obtain a pure sample of chalk?

A Warm with water—filter—evaporate the filtrate.
B Warm with water—filter—dry the filtrate.
C Warm with water—filter—dry the residue.
D Warm with water—filter—wash the residue—dry.
E Warm with water—filter—partly evaporate—allow to crystallise.

6 The solubility of naphthalene in 100 g of acetone is 67·5 g at 25°C. How many g of naphthalene will dissolve in a beaker containing 20 g of acetone at the same temperature?

A 67·5 g   B 135 g   C 6·75 g   D 13·5 g   E 16·9 g

7 Which of the following would lose weight the **least** if the same volumes are left in the same size 100 cm³ beakers for 24 hours?

A mercury   D water
B alcohol   E ether
C lead(II) iodide solution

8 Rain follows which of the following sequences?

A evaporation—condensation   D condensation—evaporation
B freezing—melting   E boiling—condensation
C condensation—vaporisation

Chapter 2   Chemical joining and separation

2.1   Elements, compounds and mixtures

1 A pupil carried out the following operations and made observations. Write notes to explain each observation.

operation	observation	notes
Fine copper powder and sulphur powder were mixed.	Nothing happened.	
Dilute sulphuric(VI) acid was added to half of the mixture.	The powders tended to float but did not change.	
The other half was heated.	Red glow. Heat given off. Black mass left.	
The black mass was treated with dilute sulphuric(VI) acid.	Blue solution. Hydrogen sulphide gas given off.	

2 A chemist heated three weighed amounts of sodium in chlorine gas and then weighed the product in each case. The following results were obtained:

	weight of sodium	weight of product	weight of chlorine
1.	2·3 g	5·75 g	
2.	3·45 g	8·625 g	
3.	1·15 g	2·875 g	

a He took the weight of sodium from the weight of product. Do this yourself and write out the third column in full.

b He worked out the percentage of each element.

$$\% = \frac{\text{weight of element} \times 100}{\text{weight of product}}$$

Do the calculation and make up a table as follows:

	% sodium	% chlorine
1.		
2.		
3.		

c What information about the product does this give?

3 List the following changes under the headings of *physical change* and *chemical change*.
   a A metal, labelled A, melted when heated. On cooling it resolidified.
   b A metal, labelled B, was added to acid. The solution became hot and effervesced.
   c Two elements, labelled C and D, were mixed together The mixture glowed and much heat was given off.
   d A solid labelled E dissolved in a solvent labelled F.
   e The solution EF was boiled. A white residue of E remained on evaporation.
   f The product from **c** was heated strongly. The element labelled D sublimed on the cooler parts of the test-tube.

4 Given the following data on a series of substances A to F, write down whether the substance indicated is **a** *metal*, **b** *non-metal*, **c** *compound*.

mp °C	bp °C	appearance	conductivity	dil. acid	oxide	a, b or c
A	801	1413	white solid	low	no action	—	
B	114	444	yellow solid	very low	no action	acidic	
C	98	885	dull solid	very high	explosive	basic	
D	1410	2680	dull solid	low	no action	acidic	
E	651	1107	shiny solid	high	hydrogen	basic	
F	d 1026		black solid	low	blue soln.	—	

5 Write down the names of the following chemicals. In separate columns enter the names of the elements composing each and give their formulae.

	element 1	element 2	element 3	formula
calcium oxide				
barium chloride				
carbon tetrachloride				
copper(II) oxide				
lead(II) bromide				
lithium oxide				
aluminium iodide				
hydrogen chloride				
copper(II) sulphide				
magnesium nitride				
silicon dioxide				
sodium fluoride				
phosphorus trichloride				
silver(I) nitrate(V)				
sodium carbonate				
copper(II) sulphate(VI)				
lead(II) nitrate(III)				
silver(I) chloride				

6 Most (but not all) of the substances in the **top** half of the table in Q. 5 can be synthesised by heating together the two elements. Answer yes/no to the following:

a All the substances are mixtures.
b It is possible to obtain pure elements from them by distillation.
c Chemical methods are necessary if pure elements are to be obtained.
d The lead in lead(II) bromide has the same properties as the pure element lead.
e The sulphur in copper(II) sulphide has the same properties as the pure element sulphur.

2.2 Heat transfer in chemical reactions

1 Heat transfers to and from the surroundings were measured during the changes described. Heat transfers **to** the surroundings were given a negative sign and heat transfers **from** the surroundings a positive sign.

A	molten tin resolidified	− 7·22 kJ mol^{-1}
B	lead melted	+ 4·78 kJ mol^{-1}
C	chloroform vaporised	+ 2·94 kJ mol^{-1}
D	calcium burning to produce calcium oxide	− 638·4 kJ mol^{-1}
E	water split into oxygen and hydrogen	+286·0 kJ mol^{-1}
F	water changed into steam	+ 41·24 kJ mol^{-1}
G	molten tin is vaporised	+289·60 kJ mol^{-1}

a Which of the above changes are exothermic?
b Which of the above changes are easily reversible?
c Which of the above changes produce a new chemical?
d Compare the heats associated with the easy reversible changes and the others. What do you notice about their magnitude?
e Is the following statement true?
Physical changes of state are accompanied by little or no change in energy?
f Which of the above liquids is the most difficult to vaporise?
g Hydrogen burns in oxygen to give water. How much heat would be given out (mol^{-1})?

2 Following is an energy profile (in heat units) of an exothermic reaction.

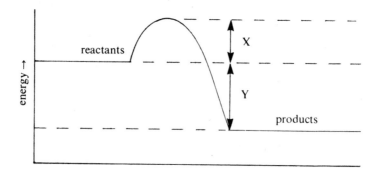

a What does the difference in energy X represent?
b What does the difference in energy Y represent?
c If a reaction occurred spontaneously what can you say about the energy difference X?
d Draw a similar profile for an endothermic reaction.

3 When new bonds are formed i.e. when a new compound is made from its elements, heat is given out. When the elements are separated from each other then heat is taken in. Which of the following are likely to be exothermic? Write down an explanation for acceptance or rejection.
  a Magnesium burning to magnesium oxide.
  b Ammonium chloride dissociating into ammonia and hydrogen chloride.
  c Heating mercury oxide to produce mercury and oxygen.
  d Heating copper to form copper(II) oxide.

2.3 Elements as metals and non-metals

1 Explain how the following circuit can be used to separate samples of metal and non-metal.

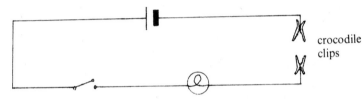

crocodile clips

2 This is a graph of mp for the lighter elements. Write down atomic numbers in answer to the following:
  a Which are solids?
  b Which are likely to be non-metals?
  c The first two peaks are carbon and silicon. Are these metals?
  d What points represent metals?

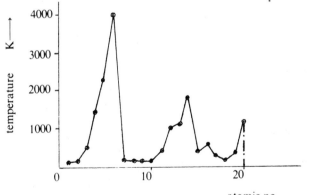

atomic no. ⟶

23

3 Write down whether or not the element X is a metal or non-metal in each of the following cases.

   a XCl_5 reacts vigorously with water producing white fumes.
   b XO_2 is an acidic gas.
   c XO_2 is a very unreactive solid.
   d XO is fairly soluble in water and alkaline.
   e XH_4 is a very inflammable gas.
   f X_2O is very acidic and reacts violently with water.
   g X_2O reacts violently with water and gives a strong alkaline solution.
   h XCl_2 is a neutral salt which dissolves in water.
   i XH is a salt-like hydride.
   j XH is an acidic gas.

4 A fine powder burned when sprinkled into a bunsen flame; gave hydrogen when added to dilute acid and turned yellow when it was heated. Answer the following questions, giving reasons for your answers.

   a Is the substance a metal, a non-metal, or a compound?
   b Does the substance melt above or below 500°C?
   c Identify the substance.

2.4 Symbols and formulae

1 Which of the following *symbols* does **not** represent an element?
   C   Cu   NO   Na   Br

2 Which of the following is **not** an element?
   phosphorus   sulphur   water   chlorine   caesium

3 Which of the following *formulae* does **not** represent a compound?
   CuO $NaCl$ CS_2 Mn CO

4 Which of the following are **not** compounds?
   hydrogen chloride   hydrogen gas   dichlorine oxide
   silver(I) nitrate(V)   ammonia

5 How many atoms of each element are indicated by the following?
   $2Na$ $5Cu$ $3C$ $6S$ $2Co$
Write down, in **words**, what the numbers and symbols say.

6 How many molecules of each compound are indicated by the following?
   $2CuO$ $4CO_2$ $3MnO_2$ $3NaCl$ $6KMnO_4$
Write down, in **words**, what the numbers and formulae say.
Write down the numbers of atoms of each element present in each formula.

7 Write down, in **words**, the number of atoms of oxygen which can be obtained by breaking down the following molecules:

$Cu(NO_3)_2$ $\quad$ $Al_2(SO_4)_3$ $\quad$ $CuSO_4 . 5H_2O$ $\quad$ $CaCO_3$ $\quad$ Na_2O_2

8 Write down the formula for each of the following:
sodium oxide $\quad$ sodium nitrate(V) $\quad$ nitrogen(IV) oxide
calcium chloride $\quad$ silicon(IV) chloride

9 Write down the formula corresponding to each named compound.
dichlorine oxide $\quad$ hydrogen sulphide $\quad$ nitrogen(III) chloride
sodium sulphate(VI) $\quad$ lead(II) nitrate(V)

10 Which of the following formulae is incorrect?
CuO $\quad$ OMn $\quad$ Cl_2O $\quad$ $NaNO_3$ $\quad$ SO_2

11 Which elemental gases do the following formulae represent?
$N_2(g)$ $\quad$ $O_2(g)$ $\quad$ $Cl_2(g)$ $\quad$ $H_2(g)$ $\quad$ $F_2(g)$
How many atoms are there in each molecule of the gases represented?

2.5 Chemical equations

1 Synthesis is the joining of two elements to form a compound.
 a Complete the following **word** equations representing synthesis.

carbon + oxygen $\longrightarrow$
sulphur + $\qquad$ $\longrightarrow$ sulphur dioxide
$\qquad$ + chlorine $\longrightarrow$ sodium chloride
$\qquad$ + $\qquad$ $\longrightarrow$ aluminium bromide
$\qquad$ + $\qquad$ $\longrightarrow$ sulphur(II) chloride

 b Write **balanced** equations for each synthesis.

2 All the formulae in the following equations are correct but the equations are unbalanced. Write **balanced** equations.

 a $SO_2 + O_2 \longrightarrow SO_3$
 b $Mg + HCl \longrightarrow MgCl_2 + H_2$
 c $NaCl + Pb(NO_3)_2 \longrightarrow NaNO_3 + PbCl_2$
 d $Na_2CO_3 + CaCl_2 \longrightarrow NaCl + CaCO_3$
 e $AlCl_3 + H_2O \longrightarrow Al(OH)_3 + HCl$

25

3 Write out in **words** what the following equations say.

   a $2NaNO_3 \longrightarrow 2NaNO_2 + O_2$

   b $2Mg + O_2 \longrightarrow 2MgO$

   c $FeS + 2HCl \longrightarrow FeCl_2 + H_2S$

   d $CuSO_4 \longrightarrow CuO + SO_3$

   e $Na_2SO_4 + Ba(NO_3)_2 \longrightarrow 2NaNO_3 + BaSO_4$

4 The following equations provide more information. Write out, in **words**, *all* the information conveyed.

   a $C(c) + O_2(g) \longrightarrow CO_2(g)$

   b $2Fe(s) + 3Cl_2(g) \longrightarrow 2FeCl_3(g)$

   c $NH_4Cl(c) \rightleftharpoons NH_4Cl(g)$

   d $CuS(c) + 2HCl(aq) \longrightarrow CuCl_2(aq) + H_2S(g)$

   e $H_2(g) + Cl_2(g) \longrightarrow 2HCl(g)$

5 When copper was heated with concentrated nitric(V) acid, a blue solution of copper(II) nitrate(V) was formed and the gas nitrogen(IV) oxide was given off. Excess water was boiled off and blue crystals collected. When the crystals were heated, copper(II) oxide formed and nitrogen(IV) oxide and oxygen were given off. Write **two** equations to represent the chemical reactions.

Objective test 2

Apply Rubric A instructions

1 Which of the following phrases would you **not** use?
   A an atom of an element   D an atom of a compound
   B a molecule of a compound ⋅ E the atoms in a compound
   C a molecule of an element

2 Which of the following can be separated into elements physically?
   A sodium bromide   D sodium mercury amalgam
   B water   E lead(II) oxide
   C alcohol

3 Which of the following changes is **not** easily reversible?
   A ice changing to water   D iodine vapour changing to solid iodine
   B salt dissolving   E magnesium and oxygen combining to
   C acetone evaporating   form magnesium oxide

4 Which of the following changes is **not** likely to give out heat?
   A water freezing
   B iron(II) sulphide being made from heating sulphur and iron filings
   C ammonium nitrate(V) dissolving
   D sulphur burning
   E an acid reacting with magnesium ribbon

5 Which of the following is not true?
   A A metal is lustrous.
   B Metals are good conductors of heat and electricity.
   C Metals burn in oxygen to form basic oxides.
   D A metal reacts with chlorine to form salts.
   E Metallic chlorides are insoluble.

6 Which of the following formulae is wrongly written?
   A $NaNO_3$ B $BaCl_2$ C SO_3 D $NaBr_3$ E CCl_4

7 Which of the following equations is unbalanced?
   A $2NaNO_3 \longrightarrow 2NaNO_2 + O_2$
   B $Al + 6HCl \longrightarrow AlCl_3 + 3H_2O$
   C $2KClO_3 \longrightarrow 2KCl + 3O_2$
   D $2Ba(NO_3)_2 \longrightarrow 2BaO + 4NO_2 + O_2$
   E $CaCl_2 + 2AgNO_3 \longrightarrow 2AgCl + Ca(NO_3)_2$

8 Two molecules of solid iron(II) sulphate(VI), when heated, give solid iron(III) oxide, one molecule of sulphur dioxide gas and one molecule of sulphur trioxide gas. Which of the following most accurately and adequately represents this statement?
   A $FeSO_4 \longrightarrow Fe_2O_3 + SO_2 + SO_3$
   B $2FeSO_4(s) \longrightarrow Fe_2O_3(s) + SO_2 + SO_3$
   C $2FeSO_4(s) \longrightarrow Fe_2O_3(s) + SO_2(g) + SO_3(g)$
   D $2FeSO_4 \longrightarrow Fe_2O_3 + SO_2 + SO_3$
   E $2FeSO_4 \longrightarrow Fe_2O_3(s) + SO_2(g) + SO_3$

Chapter 3 The particle nature of matter

3.1 How big is a molecule?

1 The following arrangement was set up in a fume cupboard.

conc. HCl   ammonia

Fumes appeared above X almost immediately. The fumes were dense.
Fumes appeared above Y after an interval. The fumes were not dense.
Explain **a** why fumes appeared
        b the difference in density.

2 In an experiment 1 g of potassium manganate(VII) was dissolved in
1 dm^3 (1000 g) of water. 100 cm^3 of this solution was taken and again
made up to 1 dm^3 with water. The process was repeated five times when
it became impossible to detect the purple colour of the manganate(VII).
  a How many g of potassium manganate(VII) remain after the fifth
    dilution?
  b If the amount found in **a** is dissolved in 1 dm^3 of water, how many
    g of potassium manganate(VII) are there per g of water?
  c What does this indicate about the smallest particle of potassium
    manganate(VII)?
  d If the actual mass of a particle of potassium manganate(VII) is
    $2 \cdot 63 \times 10^{-24}$ g, how many more times would you have to dilute the
    original 1 g per dm^3 to get down to 1 particle in 1 g water?

3 0·4 g of olive oil was dissolved in 1 dm^3 of petroleum ether. Two
drops of this solution spread over water to an area of 100 cm^2. Two
drops are equivalent to 0·1 cm^3.
  a What is the weight of olive oil in 1 cm^3 of solution?
  b What is the weight of olive oil in two drops?
  c What is the weight of olive oil in the layer of area 100 cm^2?
  d Assuming the layer is d cm thick what is its volume?
  e Calculate d assuming the density of olive oil is unity.

4 18 cm^3 of water contains 6×10^{23} particles. What is the volume of
1 particle? What is its diameter?

3.2 Movement of molecules

1 A refined version of apparatus A (opposite) is used to determine the
vapour density of gases. The tube is filled with gas from a suitable source
and the gas allowed to escape through a small pinhole. As it escapes the
water level in the tube rises.

a Which gas would escape the quickest—hydrogen or carbon dioxide?

b Nitrogen and carbon monoxide escape at the same rate. What can you say about them?

c A sample of air escaped in 28 seconds. A sample of propane took 44 seconds. Which gas is the more dense and by how much?

d Carbon dioxide is acidic and tends to dissolve in water. What would you do before carrying out the experiment with carbon dioxide?

2 Account for the following facts.

   a Very hard solids do not smell at room temperature.

   b A solid like rancid butter smells but not at a distance.

   c If a small leakage of hydrogen sulphide gas occurs in the laboratory, the whole school smells it very quickly.

   d The type of gas used in the Great War was very dangerous to both friend and foe.

   e Modern type 'war gases' are of the vaporised spray kind.

3 Consider apparatus B (below).

   a Gas X is inside the pot and gas Y outside. The manometer is as shown. Which gas is diffusing the faster?

   b Gas X is outside the pot and gas Y inside. What will be the position of the liquid in the manometer? Draw it.
   Which gas is diffusing the faster?

   c Gas W is inside the pot and gas Z outside. The levels in the manometer are exactly the same height. Which gas is diffusing the faster? Can you say anything else about them?

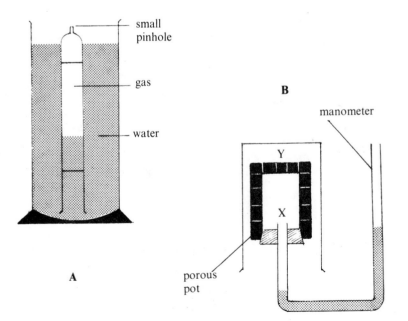

small pinhole

gas

water

A

B

manometer

Y

X

porous pot

3.3 Kinetic theory and states of matter

This section is based on the kinetic theory which may be summarised as follows:

a All matter is made up of small, separate particles.

b Above absolute zero the particles are continuously moving in some way.

c The particles are attracted to each other by electrical attractions. These attractions are called bonds.

d As more energy is added the movement of particles increases. This can be measured by the increase in temperature.

e The attractive bonds become less effective as the particles acquire more energy and move more vigorously.

f In solids, attractions predominate and the particles are held together closely. Their movement is confined mainly to vibration.

g In gases, attractions are ineffective and the particles are far apart. The movement is translational (i.e. predominantly in straight lines).

1 Solve the following hypothetical puzzles based on diffusion.

a The two gas particles are identical. Draw a diagram representing the position after the tap is opened.

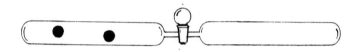

b Repeat a. This time there are two particles of another gas as well.

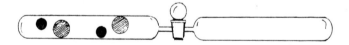

c The diagram represents two layers of liquids X and Y. Draw a diagram representing the position after thorough shaking.

d The diagram is of a manometer connected to a Buchner flask. Draw a diagram to represent the position of liquid in the manometer after the introduction of 1 drop of acetone.

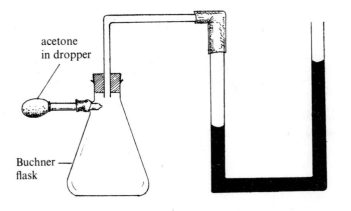

acetone
in dropper

Buchner
flask

e Refer to **d**. Draw a diagram showing the position after n, and n + 1, drops of acetone have been added (i.e. a large amount).

2 Solve the following hypothetical puzzles based on evaporation of liquid.
   a Two vessels are shown, one closed to the atmosphere and the other open. Show the position as you think it may be after some time.

   b Both spaces are closed. One contains 20 particles of water at below freezing. The other contains 20 particles of water at 200°C. Draw in the particles.

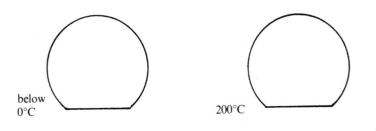

below
0°C   200°C

c The container contains a solution. The shaded particles are the solute. Draw the model of the situation after prolonged boiling.

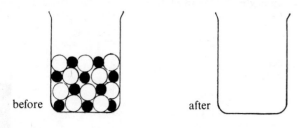

before   after

d The container contains a suspension. The suspended solid is shown shaded. Draw the position after filtration.

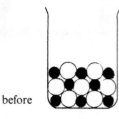 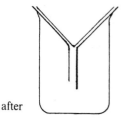

before   after

e The container contains a suspension as before. Show the position after evaporation.

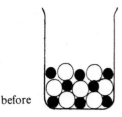 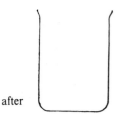

before   after

3 Solve the following hypothetical puzzles based on change of state.
  a The weak and strong springs represent the bonds holding the particles together in a solid. Which diagram represents the solid with the higher mp?

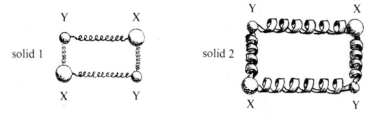

solid 1   solid 2

b Which diagram represents the solid which would need the greater amount of energy to break it up into X and Y elements?

c Represent **one** solid as it would be in the gaseous state.

d Would the average length of the springs be shorter or longer at higher temperatures?

e At what temperature would there be no vibration of the springs?

4 Solve the following hypothetical puzzles based on the gas laws.

a What is the pressure in the second case?

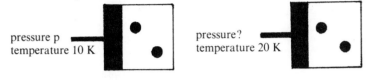

pressure p
temperature 10 K

pressure?
temperature 20 K

b What is the pressure in the second case?

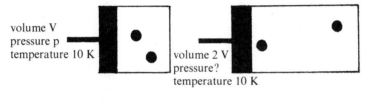

volume V
pressure p
temperature 10 K

volume 2 V
pressure?
temperature 10 K

c What is the pressure in the second case?

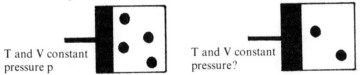

T and V constant
pressure p

T and V constant
pressure?

3.4 The chemical laws

1 In the following reactions the volume of one of the gases is indicated. Find the volume of any other gas present (all volumes measured at s.t.p.) for the balanced equation.

a $C + O_2 \longrightarrow CO_2$
     20 cm^3

b $C_3H_8 + 5O_2 \longrightarrow 3CO_2 + 4H_2O$
     15 cm^3

c $2H_2 + O_2 \longrightarrow 2H_2O$
     1 litre

2 Equal volumes of two gases A and B were mixed, and 300 cm³ of the mixture allowed to react. On completion of the reaction the total volume of gas left was 200 cm³. All the gas B had reacted but 100 cm³ of A was left mixed with a new gas C.

    a Find the volume of new gas formed.
    b Write down the reacting volumes of the gases.
    c Give a balanced equation for the reaction.

3 A gas occupies 819 cm³ at s.t.p. Complete the following table for the same mass of this gas under the new conditions indicated.

volume cm³	temperature °C	pressure mm Hg
	57	855
750		800
650	52	

Objective test 3

Apply Rubric A instructions

1 The % by weight of gold in sea water is 1.6×10^{-7}. The weight of a gold particle is 3.2×10^{-24}. Which of the following is the nearest to the number of particles of gold in 1 g of sea water?
    A 1000   B 5×10^{10} C 5×10^{14} D 5   E 5 000 000

2 Which of the following is the nearest to representing the correct diameter of an average molecule?
    A 10^{-10} B 10^{-8} C 10^{-6} D 10^{-14} E 10^{-4}

3 The gases X, Y and Z have the densities 22, 16 and 14 respectively. Which of the following is **true** of the rates of diffusion?
    A all the same   B X fastest   C Z fastest   D Y and Z the same
    E Y the fastest

4 Which statement is **untrue**?

    A The particles of a gas move faster at higher temperatures.

    B All particles of matter are in motion at temperatures above absolute zero.

    C When a gas sublimes to a solid the particles stop vibrating.

    D If a given volume of gas is compressed then the number of particles in a unit volume increases.

    E During rapid evaporation the temperature of a liquid goes down.

5 Which of the following statements is **correct** relative to light gas X and heavy gas Y?

    A At a given temperature the kinetic energy of X particles will be higher than the kinetic energy of Y particles.

    B At a given temperature the kinetic energy of both X and Y particles will be the same.

    C The kinetic energy of X and Y will only be the same at different temperatures.

    D Since the kinetic energy is $\frac{1}{2}mv^2$ the heavier particles will have more energy.

    E Since the kinetic energy is $\frac{1}{2}mv^2$ the faster particles will have more energy.

6 Which of the following is an erroneous statement of Avogadro's law?

    A Equal volumes of two gases contain the same number of molecules.

    B If two gases are at the same temperature and pressure and occupy the same volume then the volumes must contain an equal number of particles.

    C $22\cdot4$ dm^3 of gas X contains the same number of particles as $22\cdot4$ dm^3 of gas Y at the same temperature and pressure.

    D Equal volumes of two gases at the same temperature and pressure contain equal numbers of molecules.

    E Two gases at equal pressures and having the same volume and temperature contain the same number of particles.

Chapter 4   Acidity and basicity

4.1 and 4.2   Acids, bases, alkalis and pH scale

1 Write down a description of the result of the following actions performed with a dilute aqueous solution of an acid. Name any gas given off.
  a placing a little on the tip of the tongue
  b adding a little to magnesium ribbon
  c adding a little to baking powder
  d adding a little to washing soda crystals
  e adding a little to powdered chalk

2 The following solutions were tested with universal indicator and the pH read off. Indicate which solutions are weak and strong acids and which weak and strong alkalis.
  a pH 2   b pH 11   c pH 5   d pH 9   e pH 7

3 The following are suitable tests for alkalis. Write down a description of the result in each case.
  a The alkali is boiled with ammonium chloride crystals.
  b The alkali is added to red litmus solution.
  c The solution is rubbed between thumb and forefinger.
  d Universal indicator is added.

4 Alkalis are soluble bases. Some bases are insoluble. Which of the following are alkalis and which are insoluble bases?
  a sodium hydroxide   d zinc(II) oxide
  b copper(II) oxide   e potassium oxide
  c magnesium hydroxide

4.3   Salt formation

1 All bases react with acids to form salts and water. Complete the following word equations:
  a hydrochloric acid + sodium hydroxide $\longrightarrow$ +
  b sulphuric(VI) acid + excess copper(II) oxide $\longrightarrow$ +
  c nitric(V) acid + zinc(II) oxide $\longrightarrow$ +
  d carbonic acid + sodium hydroxide $\longrightarrow$ +
  e sodium hydroxide + excess sulphuric(VI) acid $\longrightarrow$ +

2 Complete the following equations:
  a $PbO + 2HCl \longrightarrow PbCl_2 +$
  b $2KOH + H_2SO_4 \longrightarrow$ +
  c $Ba(OH)_2 + H_2SO_4 \longrightarrow$ +

d $NaOH + H_2SO_4 \longrightarrow$ $+$

e $Na_2CO_3 + 2HCl \longrightarrow$ $+$ $+$

3 An acid may be defined as a substance with hydrogen particles which are replaceable by a metal particle (both are positive ions).
Name the acid associated with the following salts:

    a sodium hydrogen sulphate(VI)   **d** lithium nitrate(III)
    b calcium hydrogen carbonate   **e** calcium sulphate(IV)
    c sodium sulphide

4.4 Solubility of metal salts in water

1 Insoluble salts are best made by precipitation. Tabulate as soluble or insoluble:

    sodium salts   potassium salts   barium sulphate(VI)
    lead(II) chloride   calcium sulphate(VI)   magnesium sulphate(VI)
    iron(II) sulphide   zinc(II) carbonate

2 Indicate which two chemicals are needed to prepare the following insoluble salts:

    a calcium carbonate   **d** lead(II) iodide
    b copper(II) sulphide   **e** copper(II) carbonate
    c silver(I) chloride

4.5 Methods of preparing salts

1 The following is an account of the preparation of a salt by neutralising an acid with an insoluble basic oxide. Explain all the operations which are underlined.

    $25 \, cm^3$ of dilute sulphuric(VI) acid was put in a conical flask. Copper(II) oxide was added and the solution heated. It turned blue so more oxide was added until it was in excess. The solution was filtered. The filtrate was transferred to an evaporating dish and heated. When the volume of the solution was down to a third the dish was left to cool. The crystals were filtered and washed with a little distilled water.

2 The following is an account of the preparation of magnesium sulphate(VI) by neutralising an acid with a metal. Write it out, filling in the gaps.

    $25 \, cm^3$ of ____ acid was placed in a conical flask. Magnesium ribbon was added. The acid fizzed as ____ gas was given off. After half an hour although some magnesium ribbon remained the acid had stopped fizzing because it had been ____. The solution was decanted into an evaporating dish and ____. When the volume was down to a third the dish was cooled so that ____ ____ could separate.

3 The following is an account of the preparation of salt by titration of acid with an alkali. Answer the questions following.

One of two clean burettes was filled with dilute hydrochloric acid, the other with sodium hydroxide. 15 cm^3 of the acid was run into a flask, and sodium hydroxide added 0·5 cm^3 at a time. In between each addition a drop of solution was withdrawn and added to red litmus on a tile. If the drop stayed red further alkali was added until the drop changed blue. The solution was then evaporated to dryness on a steam bath.

a Why must the burette be clean and dry?
b Why was it necessary to test with litmus after each addition?
c Why was the addition stopped after the change to blue?
d Why was it necessary to evaporate to dryness?
e What salt was obtained?

4 The following is an account of the preparation of lead(II) chloride. Explain the reasons for the operations which are underlined.

Lead(II) nitrate(V) crystals were dissolved in 15 cm^3 of water. Dilute hydrochloric acid was added. A white precipitate formed. The sus-pension was filtered. The residue in the filter paper was washed repeatedly with cold distilled water. The residue was then redissolved in boiling water. On cooling, white crystals separated. The water was decanted and the crystals dried.

4.6 Testing for acid radicals

1 What information can you deduce from the following results of test-tube tests?

a A substance X dissolved in water readily. When acid was added there was a vigorous effervescence and the gas given off turned lime-water milky.

b A substance Y was insoluble. On adding dilute hydrochloric acid a gas smelling of bad eggs was given off.

c A substance Z dissolved in water and gave a white precipitate with barium chloride solution. The white precipitate dissolved in dilute hydrochloric acid.

d A substance W dissolved in dilute nitric(V) acid. When silver(I) nitrate(V) solution was added a yellow precipitate formed.

e A substance P was very soluble. When a crystal of iron(II) sulphate(VI) and a few drops of concentrated sulphuric(VI) acid were added a brown colour developed which quickly disappeared on shaking.

2 The laboratory technician had lost the labels off the bottles of two sodium salts. They were both white and looked identical in all respects. The two labels lost were sodium sulphate(VI) and sodium hydrogen sulphate(VI). Suggest a way in which the matter could be resolved.

Objective test 4

Apply Rubric A instructions

1 Which of the following is a **strong** acid?
A solution pH 5   D solution pH 13
B solution pH 2   E solution pH 10
C solution pH 7

2 Which of the following reactions is **not** a property of an alkali?
A soluble   D turns red litmus blue
B gives salts with acids   E liberates ammonia when boiled with
C insoluble   ammonium chloride

3 To which of the following data can the response "It's an acid" be made?
A Soluble, colourless solution, pH 12, dissolved Al powder.
B Soluble, colourless solution, pH 7.
C Solid, soluble in water. Dissolves magnesium ribbon.
D Solid, insoluble in water. Converted into salt with acid.
E Solid, sparingly soluble. Solution turned red litmus blue.

4 Which of the following is **not** a salt?
A sodium hydroxide   D copper(II) chloride
B silver(I) nitrate(V)   E aluminium sulphate(VI)
C calcium carbonate

5 Which of the following is insoluble?
A barium chloride   D silver(I) chloride
B lead(II) nitrate(V)   E sodium carbonate
C potassium sulphate(VI)

6 Which of the following salts **cannot** be made starting from any **two** of sodium hydroxide, sulphuric(VI) acid, magnesium oxide?
A magnesium sulphate(VI)   D magnesium hydroxide
B sodium hydrogen sulphate(VI)   E magnesium hydrogen
C sodium sulphate(VI)   sulphate(VI)

7 Which of the following salts **cannot** be made by direct synthesis?
A sodium chloride   D copper(II) sulphate(VI)
B aluminium chloride   E sodium hydride
C iron(II) sulphide

8 Which of the following salts **cannot** be made by precipitation methods?
A zinc(II) sulphide   D calcium carbonate
B barium sulphate(VI)   E silver(I) iodide
C zinc(II) nitrate(V)

9 Which is the best sequence for preparing crystals of a soluble salt starting with acid and metal?

A Excess acid—metal—filter—evaporate—decant—dry crystals.

B Excess metal—acid—filter—evaporate—cool—decant—dry crystals.

C Excess metal—acid—filter—wash residue.

D Excess acid—metal—filter—wash residue—redissolve—recrystallise.

E Excess metal—acid—evaporate—cool—filter—wash crystals—dry.

10 Which method is best for preparing sodium nitrate(V)?

A add sodium to nitric(V) acid

B add sodium oxide to nitric(V) acid

C add sodium hydroxide to nitric(V) acid

D add sodium to zinc(II) nitrate(V)

E heat sodium nitrate(III)

Chapter 5   The structure of atoms

5.1   The fundamental particles

1 Write out, filling in the missing words.
   a The proton has a charge of ____ and a mass of ____.
   b The neutron has a charge of ____ and a mass of ____.
   c The electron has a charge of ____ and a mass of ____.
   d If the atom is to be neutral the number of electrons must equal ____
   e The hydrogen atom has a charge of ____ and a mass of ____.

2 The apparatus shown was used by J. J. Thomson to detect negative particles. These were subsequently found to be electrons. Answer the following questions:
   a What does the ammeter reading indicate?
   b If current flowed in the direction indicated, which way did the electrons travel?
   c How might it be possible to show that these particles (called electrons) had momentum and travelled in straight lines?
   d Later, Thomson found particles travelling in the opposite direction from the anode. What might they be?
   e What did he find about the momentum of these particles relative to that of the electrons?

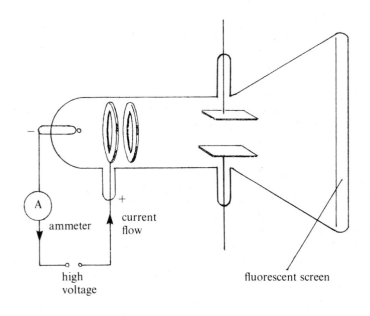

5.2 The nucleus

1 Draw the following:
   a A *nucleus* having a mass number of 12 and a charge of 6+.
   b A *nucleus* of atomic mass 24 and atomic number 12.
   c A *nucleus* containing 8 protons and 8 neutrons.

2 The following nuclei have the same atomic number but the numbers of neutral particles are different.

nucleus A	*nucleus B*
atomic number 12	atomic number 12
neutral particles 12	neutral particles 14

   a What are the mass numbers of the two nuclei?
   b What would be the approximate atomic masses of the nuclei?
   c What is the charge on the nucleus in both cases?
   d What are atoms with the same atomic number but different mass number called?
   e Assuming that normally A and B are found in the ratio of 9:1, what is the atomic mass of the element containing both nuclei?

5.3 Electron patterns

1 Write out electron configurations for the five different elements below, using only the information provided.
   a atomic number is 14
   b the atom has 10 electrons
   c the number of protons is 15
   d the symbol is Na
   e there are four shells—three have the maximum number of electrons and the fourth has two electrons

2 Complete the following statements:
   a The number of electrons in a neutral atom is equal to ____.
   b The electrons in the shells nearer the nucleus require ____ energy to be removed than the ones further away.
   c The energy shells nearer the nucleus are filled ____.
   d The maximum number of electrons in any shell is given by ____ where n is the shell number.
   e The electrons in the ____ shell are affected in chemical combination because they are more ____.

Objective test 5

Apply Rubric A instructions

Which of the following is an incorrect statement?

1 A The number of neutrons plus the number of protons is equal to the mass number.
  B The number of protons is equal to the atomic number.
  C The number of protons and neutrons is equal to the atomic mass.
  D The number of electrons is equal to the atomic number for a neutral atom.
  E The mass of protons, neutrons and electrons is equal to the atomic mass.

2 A The electron configuration of sodium is 2 8 1.
  B The electron configuration for element of atomic number 9 is 2 7.
  C The element of atomic number 10 has 8 electrons in the outer shell.
  D The electron configuration of calcium is 2 8 9 1.
  E The electron configuration of potassium is 2 8 8 1.

3 A The nucleus of carbon is approximately 2 × 1840 times heavier than the rest of the atom.
  B The amount of energy needed to split the nucleus is many million times greater than the energy needed to remove an electron.
  C All atoms of hydrogen contain one proton.
  D Every nucleus contains neutrons and protons.
  E The nuclei of the same elements must always contain the same number of protons.

4 For an atom of electron configuration 2 8 14 2
  A the total number of electrons is 26
  B the penultimate shell contains 10 electrons
  C two electrons are more easily removed than the rest
  D the total number of protons in the nucleus will be 26
  E the second shell contains a maximum number of electrons.

5 An element has atomic number 12. This is sufficient to indicate
  A the identity of the element
  B the exact number of electrons
  C the number of protons in the nucleus
  D the configuration of the electrons
  E the number of isotopes the element has.

SECTION TWO
FACTORS WHICH CONTROL
CHEMICAL REACTIONS

Chapter 6   How chemicals react

6.1   Stable, outer shell, electron arrangements

1 Write down the electronic configuration of the noble gases helium, neon, argon, krypton and xenon.

2 The following arrangement of elements is part of the periodic table. They are in order of their atomic numbers.

He	Li	Be	B	C	N	O	F	Ne
2	3	4	5	6	7	8	9	10
Na	Mg							
11	12							

a How many electrons must Na lose to have an inert-gas, electron configuration?

b How many electrons must Mg lose to have an inert-gas, electron configuration?

c How many electrons must O gain to become like neon in electron configuration?

d Why would you expect Li to be similar to Na?

e Which one would you expect to be more reactive, oxygen or fluorine?

6.2   Electrovalency

1 Write electron configurations for the atoms of N, Na, Cl, S and K.

2 Write electron configurations for the following ions:
Mg^{2+} Li^+ Al^{3+} O^{2-} S^{2-}

3 These are the atomic numbers and electron configurations of five elements. Answer the questions following.

A	B	C	D	E
2 8 6	2 8 7	2 8 8	2 8 8 1	2 8 8 2

a Which configuration represents an inert gas?

b Write down the electron configuration of the ion A^{2-}.

c Write down the electron configuration of the ion E^{2+}.

d Write down the symbol for the ion of B represented by the configuration 2 8 8.

e Write down the symbol for the ion of D represented by the configuration of 2 8 8.

4 Copy out and fill in the following table.

element	atomic no.	no. of protons	no. of electrons
Na			
Cl			
Mg			
O^{2-}			
K^+			

5 The formula of an ionic compound was X_2Y_3. Answer the following questions about this compound.

a What is the probable ionic charge on X?

b What is the probable ionic charge on Y?

c How many electrons are transferred from metal to non-metal for each molecule of X_2Y_3 formed?

d Write a balanced equation for the reaction.

e Both ions have the electronic structures 2 8. What are the electronic structures of the parent elements?

6 What do the following facts tell you?

a An element X reacted with an element Y to give a white powder.

b The substance formed had the formula XY.

c XY dissolved in water and its solution conducted electricity.

d XY gave a white precipitate when its solution was added to silver(I) nitrate(V) dissolved in nitric(V) acid.

e When XY was heated with a bunsen the flame was coloured a golden yellow.

6.3 Covalency

1 Write down and label the following as ionic or covalent.

KBr   CuS   HF H_2S SO_2

2 How many covalent bonds are associated with each of the following covalent molecules?

SCl_2 SF_6 CO_2 P_2O_3 C_2H_6

3 In which of the following is the angle between two covalent bonds the greatest, and in which is it smallest?

CO_2 H_2O NH_3 PCl_3 CH_4

4 Silicon joins with chlorine in the ratio of 1 atom of silicon to 4 atoms of chlorine.

   a Write a formula for the compound and name it.

   b Write a balanced equation for the reaction.

   c Draw a diagram showing the distribution of outer electrons in the compound.

   d How many lone pairs are there?

   e Draw a three-dimensional, structural formula showing the bond directions.

5 The following are the electron configurations of five elements.

A	B	C	D	E
2 8 2	2 8 6	2 8 8	2 8 7	2 8 3

   a Which element is unlikely to react with any of the others?

   b Which elements will react together to form covalent compounds?

   c Which elements will react to form ionic solids?

   d Which two elements will react in the ratio of 3 atoms of one to 1 atom of the other?

   e Which two atoms will give a molecule which is gaseous?

6.4 Relationship between valency type and physical properties

1 Complete the following table:

	sodium chloride	carbon dioxide
type of bonds shaken with water heated to 900°C heated to 2000°C cooled to −85°C		

2 Write out what tentative conclusions you deduce from the following:

observation	tentative conclusions
a the substance was an oily, fuming liquid **b** the substance reacted sharply with water giving copious fumes of HCl **c** the substance boiled at 75°C **d** when chlorine was bubbled through, the liquid solidified **e** the liquid did not conduct electricity	

6.5 Acids as proton donors and bases as proton acceptors

1 Consider the following compounds and list them either as *proton donors* or *proton acceptors*.

   HCl H_2O NH_3 H_2SO_3 OH^- Na_2O O^{2-}

2 Complete the following table, pairing off from this list.

H_2SO_4 OH^- HNO_3 H_2O NH_4^+ H_3O^+

Do not use the same pairing more than once.

proton donor	proton acceptor	equation
a H_2SO_4	H_2O	$H_2SO_4 + H_2O \longrightarrow H_3O^+ + HSO_4^-$
b HNO_3		
c H_3O^+		
d H_2SO_4		
e NH_4^+		

3 What is the product (products) of proton acceptance in each of the following reactions involving protons?

a $NH_3 + H^+ \longrightarrow$

b $H_2O + H^+ \longrightarrow$

c $O^{2-} + H^+ \longrightarrow$

d $SO_4^{2-} + H^+ \longrightarrow$

e $CO_3^{2-} + 2H^+ \longrightarrow$

f $Mg + 2H^+ \longrightarrow$

6.6   Ionic equations

1 Write the common ionic equation for each of the following:

a Acids reacting with divalent metals, M.

b The hydroxonium ion, H_3O^+, reacting with carbonate ions.

c The hydroxonium ion reacting with hydroxide ions.

d The silver ion, Ag^+, reacting with chloride ions.

e The barium ion, Ba^{2+}, reacting with sulphate(VI) ions.

2 Complete the following ionic equations:

a $SO_2(g) + H_2O(l) \longrightarrow$ (aq) + (aq)

b $Cu^{2+}(aq) + Zn(s) \longrightarrow Zn^{2+}(aq) +$

c $H_2SO_4(l) + 2H_2O(l) \longrightarrow$ (aq) + (aq)

d $Na_2CO_3(s) + H_2SO_4(aq) \longrightarrow$ (aq) + (l) + (g)

e $Pb(NO_3)_2(aq) + 2HCl(aq) \longrightarrow$ (s) + (aq) + (aq)

Objective test 6

Apply Rubric A instructions

1 When bromine reacts it takes up one of the following electron configurations.

A 2 8   B 2   C 2 8 8   D 2 8 18 18 8   E 2 8 18 8

2 One of the following is the electron configuration of potassium, atomic number, 19.

A 2 8 7 2   B 2 8 9   C 2 8 8 2   D 2 8 8 1   E 2 8 1

3 For an ionic compound one of the following is **untrue**.
A It has a high mp.
B It conducts electricity when molten.
C It requires quite a lot of energy to convert it to a liquid.
D It has a high solubility.
E It is composed of neutral molecules.

4 One of the following statements is in error.
A Na^+Cl^- —one electron transferred
B $(Al^{3+})_2(O^{2-})_3$ —six electrons transferred
C $Ca^{2+}Cl_2^-$ —two electrons transferred
D $Mg^{2+}O^{2-}$ —one electron transferred
E $(Na^+)_2O^{2-}$ —two electrons transferred

5 Only one of the following covalent molecules possesses two lone pairs.
A NH_3 B H_2O C BCl_3 D PCl_3 E HCl

6 One of the following possesses **one** coordinate covalent bond.
A NH_4OH B $Cu(H_2O)_4^{2+}$ C $NaOH$ D HCl E NH_3

7 The bond angles for one of the following is $109° 27'$.
A H_2O B NH_3 C PCl_5 D CH_4 E H_2S

8 One of the following is unlikely to dissolve in water.
A $NaCl$ B KNO_3 C CCl_4 D $CuSO_4$ E $MgCl_2$

9 One of the following statements is **untrue**.
A All substances containing hydrogen are acids.
B Acids neutralise all carbonates giving carbon dioxide gas.
C An acid is a proton donor to a base.
D When acids are diluted by water the water acts as a base.
E An acid reacts with many metals giving hydrogen gas.

10 Which of the following products would *precipitate* when lead(II) nitrate(V) and sodium chloride are mixed?
A lead(II) chloride
B lead(II) chloride and sodium nitrate(V)
C neither would precipitate
D sodium nitrate(V)

11 Which of the following ionic formulae is wrongly printed?
A $(Na^+)_2CO_3^{2-}$ D $Al^{3+}(Cl^-)_3$
B $Ca^{2+}(NO_3^-)_2$ E $Cu^{2+}SO_4^{2-}$
C $(K_2)^+SO_4^{2-}$

12 Which of the following **best** represents an aqueous solution of copper(II) sulphate(VI)?
A $Cu(aq) + SO_4(aq)$ D $Cu^{2+}(4H_2O) + SO_4^{2-}(aq)$
B $CuSO_4(aq)$ E $Cu^{2+}(aq) + SO_4^{2-}(aq)$
C $Cu^{2+}SO_4^{2-}(aq)$

Chapter 7   Patterns in chemical properties

7.1   Historical development

1 Newlands listed the elements as follows:

H	Li	Be	B	C	N	O	F	Na	Mg	Al	Si	P	S
Cl	K	Ca	Cr	Ti	Mn	Fe	Co	Ni	Cu				

   a What property of the elements was the basis for his list?
   b Newlands suggested a law. Write down what he called it.
   c Arrange the list so that similar elements occur periodically.
   d Where did Newlands law fall down?
   e Suggest how Newlands could have repaired the failures.

2 Classify the following elements on the basis suggested in **a** to **e** below.

H	He	Li	Be	B	C	N	O	F	Ne	Na	Mg	Al
Si	P	S	Cl	Ar	K	Ca	Ga	Ge	As	Se	Br	Kr

   a As solids, liquids and gases. List in three columns.
   b As metals, solid non-metals and gaseous non-metals. List in three columns.
   c On the basis of the number of electrons in the outside shell. List in columns 1e   2e   3e   4e   5e   6e   7e   8e.
   d On the basis of the number of shells. List in columns—1 shell, 2 shells, 3 shells and 4 shells.
   e Combine **c** and **d**, with shell number down the side and number of electrons along the top, to give a matrix.

7.2   Relationship between electron arrangement and periodic table

1 The electron arrangement for most normal (non-transition) elements can be worked out by following the arbitrary rules which refer to the periodic table.
   1 the number of shells = period number
   2 the number of outer shell electrons = group number
   3 the maximum number of electrons per shell = $2n^2$ where n = shell number
   4 the total number of electrons = atomic number

Use the periodic table to determine the electron arrangements of the following (see page 11 for periodic table).
   a Rb   **b** Se   **c** Br   **d** P   **e** Ge

2 If the electron arrangement is known then the atomic number, period number and group number can be determined. Complete the following table without reference to the periodic table.

	electron arrangement				atomic no.	period no.	group no.
A	2	8	18	3			
B	2	8	3				
C	2	8	9	2			
D	2	8	18	7			
E	2	8	18	32	4		

3 a Write out the electron arrangements for all the group 2 elements.
 b All the group 2 elements react $M \longrightarrow M^{2+} + 2e^-$. Write out the electron arrangements for all the group 2 ions, M^{2+}.
 c Write out the electron arrangements for the first **two** of the group 6 elements.
 d The group 6 elements react with metals by gaining two electrons $nM + 2e^- \longrightarrow nM^{2-}$. Write out the electron arrangements for group 6 ions, O^{2-} and S^{2-}.
 e Write out balanced equations for the reaction of M with oxygen and sulphur.

7.3 Trends across a period

1 In the short period $Na \longrightarrow Ar$ each element has an electron arrangement of three shells. Each element, successively, has one extra proton and one extra electron.
 a Which element will most easily lose an electron?
 b Which element will most easily gain an electron?
 c Which element is the most likely to share electrons?
 d Which element is the least likely to form covalent bonds?
 e Which elements are likely to form both ionic and covalent compounds?

2 Each element of the short period $Na \longrightarrow Ar$ combines with very reactive chlorine to form covalent and ionic chlorides.
 a List the elements which form covalent chlorides and write the formula for each.
 b Draw the structural formulae of any two of these chlorides.
 c Write down the ionic formulae of two chlorides of elements showing electrovalencies of $+1$ and $+3$.
 d Write down an equation for the reaction of **one** covalent chloride with water.

e Write down an ionic equation to represent a suitable chloride dissolving in water.

3 Of the elements of the short period Na ⟶ Ar, only Na, Mg and Cl react with water or steam; only Na, Mg and Al react with acid (Na explosively); and only Al, Si, P, S and Cl react with alkali.

   a What is the gaseous product of the reaction with water (steam) of Na and Mg?

   b What is the (eventual) gaseous product of the reaction of Cl_2 and water?

   c What are the gaseous products of the reactions of Na, Mg and Al with acids?

   d What is the gaseous product in the reaction of Al and alkali?

   e Write an ionic equation for the reaction of chlorine with cold alkali.

7.4 Trends down a metallic group

1 The elements of group 1 react with non-metals to form ionic compounds. They react according to the general formula $M \longrightarrow M^+ + e^-$, and the electrons are transferred to whatever reacts with the metal. Assuming the elements below receive electrons from an alkali metal, complete the ionic equations.

   a $Cl_2 + 2e^- \longrightarrow$

   b $2H_2O + 2e^- \longrightarrow$

   c $O_2 + 4e^- \longrightarrow$

   d $2H^+ + 2e^- \longrightarrow$

   e $Al^{3+} + 3e^- \longrightarrow$ (original preparation of aluminium)

2 Draw conclusions from the following observations:

observations	conclusions
a Potassium is stored in paraffin oil.	
b When a small piece of sodium is dropped in water it floats, melts and dissolves.	
c Lithium is very hard to cut with a knife. Sodium is easy to cut.	
d Potassium is always handled with dried tongs.	
e Unlike the other elements in group 1, lithium reacts only slowly in water.	

7.5 Trends in a non-metallic group

1 In group 7 the more reactive elements accept electrons from less reactive members of the same group and from other species. The general ionic reaction is $X_2 + 2e^- \longrightarrow 2X^-$ where X is any halogen. Assuming all the species below can give up electrons to a halogen, complete the ionic equations.

a $4OH^- \longrightarrow$ $+ 4e^-$
(an alkali)

b $2Na \longrightarrow$ $+ 2e^-$
(an alkali metal)

c $2Br^- \longrightarrow$ $+ 2e^-$
(a bromide)

d $2Al \longrightarrow$ $+ 6e^-$
(aluminium foil)

e Writing Cl_2 (chlorine) for X_2 write a full ionic equation for its reaction with sodium bromide.

2 The halogens also react to form covalent compounds; they share electrons with other species.
a Write an equation for the reaction of any one halogen with hydrogen.
b Write an equation for the reaction of chlorine with turps, $C_8 H_8$.
c Write an equation for the reaction of phosphorus with iodine.
d Write an equation for the reaction of chlorine with H_2S.
e Write an equation for the reaction of iodine with the thiosulphate(VI) ion $(S_2O_3{}^{2-})$.

3 Answer the following short questions.
a Why do the halogens get progressively less reactive down the group?
b Why does HI split up very easily but HCl does not?
c Why is more energy given out when fluorine reacts with hydrogen than when bromine reacts with hydrogen?
d Why do all chlorides give a white precipitate with silver(I) nitrate(V)?
e Why, when the halogens get progressively **less** reactive down a group, do the alkali metals get progressively **more** reactive down the group?

Objective test 7

Apply Rubric A instructions

1 Which of the following has the electron arrangements of a group 2 element?
    A 2 8 12 2   B 2 8 18 2   C 2 8 8 2   D 2 8 18 6   E 2 8 6

2 Which of the following has the electron configuration of a transition element?
    A 2 8 8 1   B 2 8 18 3   C 2 8 8 2   D 2 8 7   E 2 8 14 2

3 Which one of the following is **not** a good example of Döbereiner's triads?

A chlorine	35	B lithium	7	C oxygen	16
bromine	80	sodium	23	sulphur	32
iodine	127	potassium	39	selenium	79

D chromium	52	E calcium	40
iron	56	strontium	88
nickel	59	barium	137

4 Which of the following oxides is basic?
    A MgO B SiO_2 C P_2O_5 D SO_3 E Cl_2O

5 Which of the following hydrides has salt-like properties?
    A LiH B SiH_4 C PH_3 D H_2S E HCl

6 Which of the following elements is the most reactive?
    A Li   B Na   C K   D Rb   E Cs

7 Which of the following pairs of elements will react most vigorously?
    A Cs and I_2 B Rb and F_2 C Li and Cl_2 D Cs and F_2
    E Na and F_2

8 One of the following statements is untrue. Which?
    A When chlorine is bubbled into iodide solution iodine appears.
    B When bromine is added to chloride solution chlorine is formed.
    C When bromine is added to iodide solution iodine appears.
    D When chlorine is bubbled into bromide solution bromine appears.
    E When chlorine water is added to sodium bromide solution bromine appears.

9 With which of the following elements will chlorine form a tetravalent, covalent compound?
    A Cs   B Al   C Si   D P   E Ca

10 One of the following statements about the periodic table is untrue. Which?
    A The most reactive metals are found in the top left corner.
    B The most reactive gases are found in the top right corner.
    C All the transition elements are in the metallic section of the table.
    D Along a period the elements get progressively more non-metallic.
    E Down a group the elements get progressively more metallic.

Chapter 8   How much will react?

8.1   Atomic and molecular mass

1 Explain clearly what is meant by the statement that the atomic mass of sodium is 22·9.

2 Calculate the molecular mass of the following:
   a CaO   **b** $MgCl_2$ **c** $Cu(NO_3)_2$ **d** $Al_2(SO_4)_3$

8.2   The mole

1 Amounts of bricks are sold in units called a pannard. A pannard of bricks has 400 elementary units i.e. bricks. The heavy blue Staffordshire bricks weigh 1600 kg per pannard. The lighter, common bricks weigh 1200 kg per pannard.
   a A lorry full of common bricks is found to weigh 12 000 kg. How many pannards of bricks was the lorry carrying?
   b A man orders 1000 bricks. How many pannards is he ordering? What other information would he have to give to the supplier?
   c A contractor orders 11 pannards of Staffordshire bricks. How big a weight will he have to shift?
   d The diagrams represent loads of bricks on lorries. Load 1 is of Staffordshire brick and load 2 of commons. Are the lorries carrying the same load?

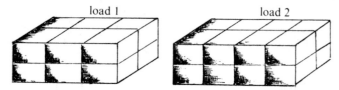

load 1   load 2

2 Amounts of particles are measured in units called the mole. A mole of particles has $6·02 \times 10^{23}$ elementary units i.e. particles. One mole of magnesium weighs 24 g. One mole of sulphur weighs 32 g.
   a A plastic beaker of negligible mass contained magnesium powder and it was found that the powder weighed 240 g. How much magnesium is this in mol?
   How much would the same beaker and contents weigh carrying the same mol of sulphur?
   b A statement is made that a beaker contains $12·04 \times 10^{23}$ particles of magnesium. What amount is this in mol?
   c A chemist decides to dissolve in acid an amount of magnesium = 10 mol. How much magnesium would have to be weighed out?
   d Two separate beakers contain magnesium and sulphur. By weighing it is found that they contain 8 mol and 6 mol respectively. Do the beakers contain the same weight of magnesium and sulphur?
   e How many particles are there in each beaker?

3 0·24 g of magnesium powder was dissolved in sulphuric(VI) acid and the resulting solution evaporated to give crystals of magnesium sulphate(VI), $MgSO_4$ $7H_2O$.

  a What is the molecular mass of $MgSO_4$ $7H_2O$?
  b Write down the ratio of molecular mass of magnesium sulphate(VI) (hydrated) to the atomic mass of magnesium.
  c Work out by simple proportions the weight of magnesium sulphate(VI) crystals formed from 0·24 g of magnesium.
  d What amount of magnesium in mol is dissolved?
  e What amount of $MgSO_4$ $7H_2O$ in mol is formed?

4 1·44 g of an oxide of copper was heated in a stream of hydrogen. The oxide was converted into 1·28 g of copper.

  a What mass of oxygen was removed from copper oxide?
  b What amount of oxide is this in mol?
  c What amount of copper was left (mol)?
  d What is the ratio of the amount of copper to the amount of oxide with which it was combined?
  e Write a formula for copper oxide which reflects this ratio.

8.3 Quantities of chemicals in solution and molarity

0·01 mol of sodium chloride in solution was added to excess silver(I) nitrate(V) solution. A precipitate of silver(I) chloride formed.

  a Write an equation for the reaction.
  b What is the ratio of sodium chloride (mol)/silver(I) chloride (mol)?
  c What amount of silver(I) chloride is formed (mol)?
  d What mass of silver(I) chloride is formed (g)?
  e What mass of sodium chloride was added initially (g)?

8.4 Titration of solutions

A pupil set out to make sodium sulphate(VI) using a solution of 0·1 M sulphuric(VI) acid and a solution of 0·05M sodium hydroxide.
He placed sodium hydroxide in a burette and 25 cm³ of 0·1 M sulphuric(VI) acid in a flask.

  a Write a balanced equation for the reaction.
  b Calculate the amount of sulphuric(VI) acid transferred to the flask (mol).
  c Work out (using mol ratio) the amount of sodium hydroxide needed to neutralise it (mol).
  d How many cm³ of the sodium hydroxide solution is this?
  e What will be the maximum weight (g) of sodium sulphate(VI) that the pupil might hope for?

8.5 The molar volume of a gas

1 A mixture of carbon monoxide and hydrogen, called synthesis gas, can be made by passing North Sea gas (methane) and steam over a nickel catalyst at 900°C. The equation is

$$CH_4(g) + H_2O(g) \longrightarrow CO(g) + 3H_2(g)$$

    a How many m^3 of steam would be needed to convert 1000 m^3 of methane into synthesis gas?

    b What would be the total volume of synthesis gas which would result?

    c What would be the total volume of gas formed from burning this synthesis gas?

    d What mass of water (kg) would have to be evaporated to create the amount of steam to make the synthesis gas?

    e What mass of steam would eventually be produced in burning the synthesis gas (kg)? (Molar volume of gas 22·4 dm^3 at s.t.p.)

2 The following apparatus was used to determine the atomic mass of magnesium in a school experiment.

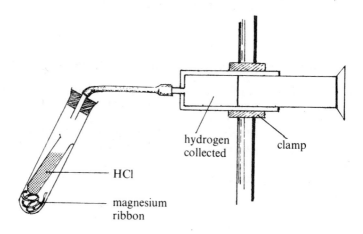

30 cm^3 of 0·1M HCl was placed in the smaller ignition tube and 0·03 g of magnesium ribbon was weighed out and placed as shown. By inverting the test-tube the magnesium reacted with the acid and the hydrogen given off was collected. It amounted to 30 cm^3.

    a Write an equation for the reaction.

    b How much magnesium was used up (mol)? (Use the symbol A for atomic mass of Mg.)

    c The molar volume of a gas is 22·4 dm^3 at s.t.p. What fraction of a molar volume is 30 cm^3?

    d By simple proportion work out A.

    e If the actual temperature of hydrogen was 27°C and the pressure 1 atmosphere, by what fraction does this result need to be corrected to get a more accurate value for A?

3 The percentage purity of chalk may be estimated in the laboratory as follows.

Weigh out accurately about 2 g of chalk and place in a conical flask. Add 50 cm^3 of 1M HCl solution. After the effervescence has ceased, boil, cool, and then titrate with 0·2M NaOH, using methyl orange as an indicator.

In such an experiment the following results were obtained:

weight of calcium carbonate   2·328 g
cm^3 of 1M HCl added   50
cm^3 of 0·2M NaOH added   40·5

a Write an equation for the reaction between chalk and HCl.
b What amount of HCl was added (mol)?
c Write an equation for NaOH reacting with HCl and determine what amount of the added HCl had reacted (mol).
d Determine the amount of $CaCO_3$ actually present (mol) as indicated by the titration.
e Determine the actual amount of $CaCO_3$ (g) and hence the percentage of the original amount which is actually calcium carbonate.

Objective test 8

Apply Rubric A instructions

1 Which of the following represents 0·1 mol calcium carbonate?
  A 10 g calcium carbonate   D 0·1 g calcium carbonate
  B 100 g calcium carbonate   E 50 g calcium carbonate
  C 1 g calcium carbonate

2 Which of the following is untrue?
  A 0·1 mol MgO (4 g MgO)   D 16 g O_2 (0·5 mol O_2)
  B 0·23 g Na (0·01 mol Na)   E 2 g H_2 (2 mol H_2)
  C 71 g Cl_2 (1 mol Cl_2)

3 Which of the following **does not** represent 0·5 mol N_2?
  A 11·2 dm^3 N_2 D 22·4 dm^3 N_2
  B 14 g N_2 E 11 200 cm^3 N_2
  C 0·014 kg N_2

4 Which of the following occupies a space of 5·6 dm^3 at s.t.p.?
  A 0·5 mol CO_2 D 0·25 mol CO_2
  B 44 g CO_2 E 1 mol CO_2
  C 22 g CO_2

5 Which of the following requires 50 cm^3 of 0·1M NaOH to neutralise?
  A 50 cm^3 0·1M H_2SO_4 D 25 cm^3 0·2M H_2SO_4
  B 25 cm^3 0·1M H_2SO_4 E 100 cm^3 0·05M H_2SO_4
  C 100 cm^3 0·1M H_2SO_4

6 Which of the following statements is untrue?

A 2(Cu), the number of moles of Cu.

B A mol is a physical quantity.

C A mol is an amount of substance.

D A mol is not a number.

E $2Cu = 2$ mol.

7 A mol of any substance is associated with 6×10^{23} particles of that substance. Which of the following represents 6×10^{21} particles?

A 0·5 mol electrons   D 100 mol Ag^+ ions

B 0·1 mol SO_4^{2-} ion   E 0·01 mol $CHCl_3$

C 10 mol C atoms

8 Which of the following is not a true statement about molecular mass?

A Molecular mass is a dimensionless number.

B The molecular mass of sodium hydroxide is 40.

C Molecular mass is a physical quantity, and has the same dimensions as the mol.

D Molecular mass of a compound is the same numerically as the mass of 1 mol of the same compound in g.

E Molecular mass is the average mass per formula unit of the natural isotopic composition relative to 1/12 the mass of an atom ^{12}C.

9 Which of the following corresponds to 0·05 mol?

A 50 cm^3 of 1M H_2SO_4 D 25 cm^3 of 2M NaOH

B 100 cm^3 of 1M H_2SO_4 E 50 cm^3 of 2M NaOH

C 50 cm^3 of 0·1M NaOH

Chapter 9   Energy and chemical reactions

9.1   Where does the energy of a chemical reaction come from?

Bond behaviour can be likened to the behaviour of an elastic band.
Consider the hypothetical example:
To break an elastic band of 10 cm requires a force of 10 g.
  a A 1 g mass is suspended from the band. How much extra force will be
     needed to break it?
  b A weight of 5 g is added. How much extra force is needed to break it?
  c The elastic band stretches 1 cm for each 1 g added. It is caused to
     oscillate between 5 cm length and 15 cm length. What force would be
     required to break it if the force was applied when it was 15 cm long?
  d In c what is the 'internal energy' stored in the stretched band when
     1 it is just about to break
     2 it is 15 cm long?
  e What will the energy be transferred to assuming the band breaks when
     the 5 g mass is suspended from it?

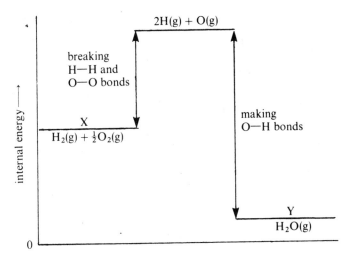

Compare the band example with the reaction $H_2(g) + \frac{1}{2}O_2(g) \rightarrow H_2O(g)$.
Refer to the diagram.
  f Which of systems X and Y has the greater potential for giving out
     energy and doing work assuming both can drop to a hypothetical
     zero internal energy?
  g Which requires the addition of most energy to it to convert it into H
     and O atoms?
  h Which of systems X and Y is the more stable (i.e. has least capacity
     for doing work)?
  i Which are the stronger bonds, H—H, O—O or O—H?

9.2 Profile of a chemical reaction

1 Answer the following questions about the diagram below.
   a What does the distance X represent?
   b What does the distance Y represent?
   c What does the distance Z represent?
   d Is the reaction exothermic or endothermic?
   e What are the units of measurement along the y axis?

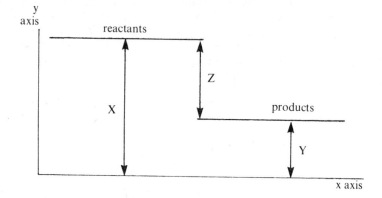

2 Answer the following questions about the diagram below.
   a What does the distance A represent?
   b What does the distance B represent?
   c If X and Y were $H^+(aq)$ and $OH^-(aq)$, respectively, in amounts
   of 1 mol, what would B represent?
   d If X and Y were carbon and oxygen, in 1 mol amounts, what would
   B represent?
   e Would B be greater for case **c** or for case **d**?

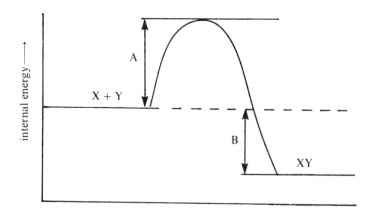

9.3 Units of energy change

1 2 g of carbon is burned in excess oxygen to form carbon dioxide with the evolution of 66 kJ of heat. Find the heat of combustion of carbon.

2 Below are the equations for chemical reactions involving ethane, ethene, and ethyne. Draw up an energy diagram and place each compound on the diagram in the correct position.

$$C_2H_2 + H_2 \longrightarrow C_2H_4; \ \Delta H - 175 \text{ kJ mole}^{-1}$$
$$C_2H_4 + H_2 \longrightarrow C_2H_6; \ \Delta H - 137 \text{ kJ mole}^{-1}$$

From the diagram find the energy change which occurs when ethyne is converted to ethane.

9.4 Types of energy change

1 In an experiment, 22·4 dm^3 of hydrogen at s.t.p. was burned, in a large vessel containing an excess of air, to form steam. The reaction was accompanied by the evolution of 243 000 J of heat.
   a Write an equation for the reaction which occurred.
   b What was the amount of hydrogen burned (mol)?
   c What was the amount of steam produced (mol)?
   d What was the volume of steam produced (dm^3 at s.t.p.)?
   e What is the value for the heat of combustion of hydrogen?
   f What is the value for the heat of formation of steam?
   g Will the heat of formation of water be less or more than the value for steam?

2 The following table is taken from the *Nuffield Book of Data*:

hydrocarbon		heat of combustion kJ mol^{-1}
methane	CH$_4$	890
ethane	C$_2$H$_6$	1560
propane	C$_3$H$_8$	2220
butane	C$_4$H$_{10}$	2877
pentane	C$_5$H$_{12}$	3509

   a Which has the highest heat of combustion *per g*?
   b Draw graphs
      1 of heat of combustion kJ mol^{-1} against number of C atoms
      2 of heat of combustion per g (kJ g^{-1}) against number of C atoms.
   c Which hydrocarbon is the most valuable fuel on a weight-for-weight basis?
   d What are the increments in heat of combustion (kJ mol^{-1}) for each —CH$_2$— group added to a molecule? Why do you think the increments go down as the molecules get bigger?
   e What are the relative advantages of North Sea gas as compared with bottled or liquefied gas?

3 The following graphs were obtained when 100 cm^3 of water and 100 cm^3 of chloroform were heated successively, but separately, in the apparatus shown.

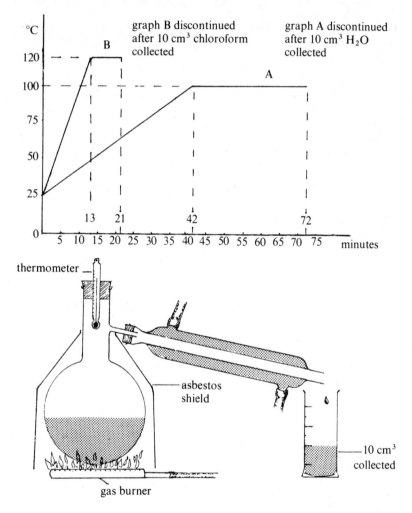

a Work out, from graph A, the amount of heat delivered by the heater per minute assuming that it requires 4·2 J to heat 1 cm^3 of water 1°C.

b Work out, from graph A, how much heat was utilised in boiling off 10 cm^3 of water at 100°C.

c Calculate the molar heat capacity of water i.e. the amount of heat needed to boil off an amount of water = 1 mol of water.

d Repeat steps **b** and **c** for chloroform, using graph B.

e Why is the graph steeper for chloroform when the amount of heat supplied per minute is the same in both cases?

4 A pupil worked out the heat of solution of ammonium chloride by weighing out 0·1 mol of the salt and dissolving it in 100 cm^3 of water in a stoppered vacuum flask. He noted the temperature of the water before adding, and its minimum after adding. The decrease was 4°C. The specific heat of water is 4·2 J cm^{-3} °C^{-1}.

   a Calculate the heat of solution of ammonium chloride.
   b Specify the units of measurement, in full.
   c Explain why the temperature went down.
   d Will the solution freeze when it drops below 0°C?
   e What might be the disadvantage of using ammonium chloride as an antifreeze?

5 50 cm^3 1M HCl was neutralised by the addition of 50 cm^3 of 1M NaOH. The addition was carried out in a vacuum flask. At the onset both solutions were at 20°C. After mixing the temperature rose to 27°C. Taking the heat capacity of water as 4·17 J g^{-1}°C^{-1} work out

   a the amount by which the heat content of the combined solutions is increased
   b the quantity in mol of H$^+$(aq) [or OH$^-$(aq)] ions neutralised
   c the heat of neutralisation.
   d The experiment was repeated with 1M HBr and 1M NaOH; and with 1M HNO$_3$ and 1M NaOH with precisely the same results in both cases. Explain why.
   e When the experiment was carried out using 1M HCl and 1M NH$_3$(aq) a result smaller by some 10% was obtained. Suggest an explanation.

Objective test 9

Apply Rubric A instructions

1 Which of the following will **not** produce an increase in temperature in the object underlined?
   A Stirring up <u>water</u> vigorously with a paddle.
   B Rubbing two <u>sticks</u> together vigorously.
   C Lifting a <u>1 kg weight</u> to the top of a tall tower.
   D Adding acid to alkali to form a <u>salt solution</u>.
   E Striking a <u>nail</u> with a hammer into a hardwood block.

2 Which of the following changes is exothermic?
   A melting ice   D dissolving salt
   B boiling water   E splitting carbon monoxide into
   C synthesising carbon dioxide   carbon and oxygen

3 0·1 M NaOH is reacted with 0·1 M HCl using 50 cm^3 volumes of each. Which is the correct value for the heat given out, given that the heat of neutralisation is 58 kJ mol^{-1}?

A 5·8 kJ   D 0·058 kJ
B 2·9 kJ   E 0·29 kJ
C 0·029 kJ

4 Which of the following is **not** true of an endothermic reaction?
A The internal energy of the reactants is greater than that of the products.
B The activation energy is higher than the internal energies of both reactants and products.
C The internal energy of the products is greater than the internal energy of the reactants.
D Heat is taken in by the system from the surroundings.
E The difference between the internal energies of reactant and products is the heat of reaction.

5 When 1 g of sulphur is burned in oxygen 9280 J of heat is given out. Which is the correct value for heat of formation of sulphur dioxide?
A 9280 kJ mol^{-1} D 29·7 kJ mol^{-1}
B   297 kJ mol^{-1} E   594 kJ mol^{-1}
C 2970 kJ mol^{-1}

6 Which of the following is **not** true of a 'spontaneous' reaction?
A Its activation energy is small.
B It cannot be stopped under normal conditions.
C It can be an exothermic or endothermic reaction.
D It can be very fast, or very slow.
E It can be reversed given the right conditions.

7 Which of the following is likely to have the highest heat of combustion?
A C_4H_{10} B CH_4 C C_5H_{12} D C_8H_{18} E C_2H_6

8 Which of the following will have the highest heat of formation?
A Na_2O B MgO C Al_2O_3 D SiO_2 E P_4O_{10}

Chapter 10   Chemical equilibria and rates of reaction

10.1   Reversibility of reactions

1 a The melting of salt is a reversible physical change. Write a reversible equation for it.
  b What conditions are likely to favour the forward reaction?
  c Is energy taken in or given out in the reverse reaction?
  d Write a similar reversible equation for salt dissolving.
  e What condition is necessary to get the salt back again?

2 a The burning of sodium in chlorine is not normally considered reversible. Write an equation for the change.
  b When sodium chloride is electrolysed sodium and chlorine separate. Write an equation for the change.
  c In what way are the conditions for reaction **a** different from the conditions for reaction **b**?
  d In what way do the energy changes associated with reactions **a** and **b** differ?
  e What would you end up with if you mixed sodium and chlorine at a temperature of 2000°C?

3 Explain the following changes by writing the appropriate reversible equations.
  a A test-tube full of iodine vapour is plunged into ice. The purple colour disappears. The test-tube is heated to 81°C. The purple colour reappears.
  b A test-tube full of brown nitrogen dioxide gas is heated to over 500°C in a bunsen flame. It becomes colourless and would relight a glowing splint. On cooling the brown colour reappears.
  c When the sun comes up the fog 'disappears'. When the sun goes down it reappears again.
  d If iron is left lying around it rusts. If the rust is heated with carbon, iron is formed.
  e Hard water is caused by calcium carbonate dissolving in carbonic acid. When hard water is heated in a kettle calcium carbonate deposits as 'fur'.

10.2 Chemical equilibrium

1 Consider the following hypothetical example:

  a A beaker contains 100 mol of a reactant X. Every minute half of the mol gets changed into a product. Draw the shape of the curve of mol of reactant plotted against minutes.

  b Assume that the rate of the reaction can be determined by drawing a tangent to the curve. Find the rate of reaction after 1 minute, 2 minutes, 3 minutes, 4 minutes and 5 minutes.

  c Draw a graph of calculated rate against concentration. What can you say about the relationship between rate and concentration?

  d Now look at the product. Let us assume 1 mol of product Y is formed for each 1 mol of reactant changed. Draw a curve of mol product against minutes on the same graph paper and same axis as for **b**.

  e In an actual reaction both **a** and **d** are taking place. How will this affect the shape of all the curves you have drawn?

2 State Le Chatelier's principle.

You are given the following information about a reaction in the gas phase:

$$H_2O(g) + C(s) \rightleftharpoons CO(g) + H_2(g); \Delta H + 22 \text{ kJ mol}^{-1}, \text{ endothermic.}$$

  a Would the per cent products be favoured by high or low temperatures?

  b Would the per cent products be favoured by high pressure?

  c What would be the effect of taking away the products as they are formed?

  d What would be the effect of passing an increased concentration of steam over the coke   1 on the concentration of products
                                            2 on the temperature of the coke?

3 Explain the following:

  a Ice melts under the pressure of a skater's skate.

  b Water boils at 20°C when the pressure is reduced sufficiently.

  c Heat always flows from a hot body to a cold body.

  d The addition of conc. HCl to saturated salt solution precipitates salt.

  e The concentration of carbon dioxide in the air stays at 0·03%.

10.3 Reaction rate

The rate of reaction of powdered calcium carbonate with 0·1 M HCl was determined at three separate temperatures, 20°C, 30°C and 40°C. x grams of calcium carbonate were used and the volume of carbon dioxide given off was measured at suitable intervals.

  a Draw a suitable apparatus for carrying out the experiment and mention any precautions which may have to be taken.

  b After 20 seconds the volumes produced at the three temperatures were 20, 40 and 80 cm³ respectively. What deduction would you make about the effect of temperature on reaction rate?

c What do you think the volume of gas might be at 50°C?
d After 1 minute the volumes were 180, 224 and 224 cm^3 respectively. What do you deduce from this?
e Calculate the value of x.

10.4 Factors which affect chemical reaction rates

1 State how the rates of the following reactions can be increased other than by raising the temperature. Give reasons for your answers.
   a the action of hydrochloric acid on marble
   b the reaction between hydrogen and chlorine
   c the decomposition of hydrogen peroxide

2 When zinc reacts with dilute sulphuric(VI) acid, hydrogen is evolved. It is suggested that perhaps copper can be used as a catalyst for the reaction. Describe experiments which would demonstrate whether copper catalyses this reaction or not.

Objective test 10

Questions 1–8   Apply Rubric A instructions

1 Which of the changes A–E is normally considered reversible?
   A two gases mixing
   B sodium sulphate(VI) dissolving in water
   C magnesium burning
   D potassium nitrate(V) thermally decomposing to oxygen
   E iron rusting

2 Which change will have no effect on the position of equilibrium of the reaction $N_2(g) + 3H_2(g) \rightleftharpoons 2NH_3(g)$; $\Delta H - 46$ kJ mol^{-1}?
   A increasing the pressure in the reaction vessel
   B decreasing the pressure in the reaction vessel
   C adding a suitable catalyst
   D increasing the temperature
   E increasing the concentration of nitrogen and hydrogen

3 Which will have no effect on the rate of the forward reaction in the equilibrium $CaCO_3(s) \rightleftharpoons CaO(s) + CO_2(g)$; $\Delta H + 179$ kJ mol^{-1}?
   A removing CO_2 as soon as it is formed
   B increasing the initial amount of $CaCO_3$
   C increasing the pressure of CO_2 by carrying out the reaction in an enclosed vessel
   D increasing the concentration of CO_2
   E increasing the temperature

4 In which of the following reactions would the position of equilibrium be unchanged with increase in pressure?

A $CO_2(g) + C(s) \rightleftharpoons 2CO(g)$

B $C(s) + H_2O(g) \rightleftharpoons H_2(g) + CO(g)$

C $3Fe(s) + 4H_2O(g) \rightleftharpoons Fe_3O_4(s) + 4H_2(g)$

D $4NH_3(g) + 5O_2(g) \rightleftharpoons 4NO(g) + 6H_2O(g)$

E $2SO_2(g) + O_2(g) \rightleftharpoons 2SO_3(g)$

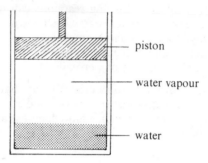

piston

water vapour

water

5 Refer to the diagram. Which process will lead to a change in pressure at equilibrium?

Note—assume that after any change the system is given time to reach equilibrium.

A decreasing the volume of water vapour by moving the piston down

B increasing the volume of water vapour by moving the piston up

C adding a *little* more water but leaving the volume of water vapour the same

D removing water but leaving the volume of water vapour the same

E increasing the temperature

6 The following reactions all started at the same time. Which produced the largest volume of gas in the first 20 seconds?

A 1 g lump of Mg in 20 cm³ of 0·1M H_2SO_4

B 1 g Mg powder in 20 cm³ of 0·1M H_2SO_4

C 1 g Mg ribbon in 20 cm³ of 0·1M H_2SO_4

D 0·5 g Mg powder in 20 cm³ of 0·1M H_2SO_4

E 1 g Mg powder in 10 cm³ of 0·2M H_2SO_4

7 When 2M HCl is added to marble chips which of the conditions following will **not** change the rate of reaction?

A using twice as much 2M HCl

B heating the solution

C powdering the chips before adding acid

D doubling the concentration of HCl

E halving the concentration of HCl

8 Which of the following is the best definition of a catalyst?

A It speeds up a reaction.

B It speeds up a reaction and sometimes takes part in it.

C It changes the rate of the reaction but is not used up in the reaction.
D It changes the rate but does not take part in the reaction.
E It changes the rate by making a path of lower energy available for the reaction.

Questions 9–23   Apply Rubric B instructions

The possibilities for the equilibrium between saturated copper(II) sulphate(VI) and concentrated hydrochloric acid are shown by the ionic equilibrium:

$$Cu(H_2O)_4{}^{2+} + 4Cl^-(aq) \rightleftharpoons CuCl_4{}^{2-}(aq)$$

blue   colourless   brown

The colour change possibilities are
  A blue to brown   D colourless to green
  B brown to blue   E brown to green
  C blue to green

What happens in the following cases?

9 Concentrated HCl is added in excess to copper(II) sulphate(VI) solution.

10 The result of Q. 9 is diluted slightly with water.

11 The result of Q. 9 is diluted heavily with water.

12 1 cm^3 of copper(II) sulphate(VI) solution is added to 10 cm^3 of conc. HCl.

13 Copper(II) sulphate(VI) solution and conc. HCl are mixed in 50/50 proportions.

The rate of reaction of dilute hydrochloric acid with sodium thiosulphate (VI) solution, to give a milky precipitate of sulphur, was studied by seeing how long it took for a black spot to disappear when viewed through the solution. In each case the volume of solution was 50 cm^3 and the same flask was used. The times were as follows
  A 10 sec   B 150 sec   C 300 sec   D 225 sec   E 75 sec

14 Which time represents the lowest concentration of sodium thio-sulphate(VI) used?

15 Which time represents the highest rate of reaction?

16 Which time represents a rate approximately twice as fast as the rate represented by time B?

17 Which time represents a rate twice as fast as the lowest rate?

18 Which time represents the next to slowest rate?

Reactions may be speeded up by
    A light
    B increase in concentration of reactants
    C increase in temperature
    D increase in pressure (for gaseous reactions)
    E catalysts.
Indicate the method used to speed up the following:

19 $NaCl(aq) \longrightarrow NaCl(s) + H_2O(g)$

20 $CH_4(g) + Cl_2(g) \longrightarrow CH_3Cl(l) + HCl(g)$

21 $2H_2O_2(l) \longrightarrow 2H_2O(l) + O_2(g)$

22 $3H_2(g) + N_2(g) \longrightarrow 2NH_3(g)$

23 $Mg(s) + 2HCl(aq) \longrightarrow MgCl_2(aq) + H_2(g)$

Questions 24–25   Apply Rubric C instructions

24 Le Chatelier's principle may be stated as follows:
    1 Changing the external conditions of any system in equilibrium causes the equilibrium to adjust to accommodate the changes.
    2 Nature abhors a vacuum.
    3 Any change leads to adjustment and accommodation.
    4 Any change is opposed and prevented.

25 When deep brown N_2O_4 gas is slowly warmed it becomes light brown, then colourless because
    1 it decomposes to $NO(g)$ and $O_2(g)$, both of which are colourless
    2 it decomposes to light brown $NO_2(g)$, then to colourless $N_2(g)$ and $O_2(g)$
    3 it decomposes to light brown $NO_2(g)$, then to $NO(g)$ and $O_2(g)$, both of which are colourless
    4 it decomposes gradually to colourless $NO_2(g)$.

Chapter 11   Electrochemistry

11.1   Electrical conductivity and chemicals

1 An electrolysis was carried out in a U-tube as shown in diagram A.
The tube was rocked from time to time during the experiment.

   a Why did the water change colour from green to deep blue?

   b Explain why the colour in the brine compartment changed from green
to pinkish to colourless as the reaction proceeded.

   c Write an equation for the reaction taking place at the mercury in the
brine compartment.

   d Write an equation for the reactions at the anode.

   e Why is the tube rocked?

   f What is the eventual product of the brine compartment and water
compartment respectively?

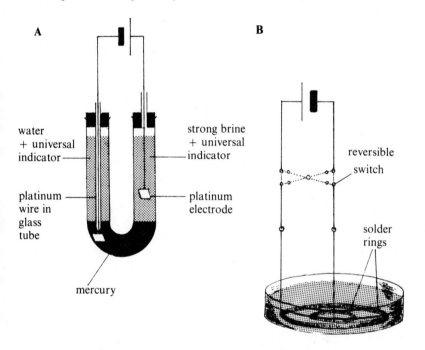

A

water
+ universal
indicator

platinum
wire in
glass
tube

mercury

strong brine
+ universal
indicator

platinum
electrode

B

reversible
switch

solder
rings

2 The spirals of solder (tin/lead alloy) are immersed in tin(II) chloride
solution in concentrated HCl in a shallow petri dish. A battery is connected
via a reversible switch (diagram B). Explain the following:

   a As the current is switched on there is a rapid growth of crystals of
tin from the centre outwards.

   b As the current is reversed the crystals diminish inwards.

   c As the crystals diminish inwards new crystals grow from the outer
electrode. Write an equation for the reactions.

11.2 Electrolysis

1 0·02 Faraday was passed through a solution of sodium hydroxide using platinum electrodes.
   a Draw a labelled diagram of a suitable apparatus for the collection of products in a realistic length of time.
   b Write down the names of the products at each electrode.
   c Represent the reactions at the electrodes with ionic equations.
   d Calculate the mol of products released at each electrode, and also the volume, where the product is a gas.
   e Calculate the time required to complete the passage of 0·02 F if the current is 2 amps.

2 Solutions of various salts in water were electrolysed and the number of Faradays needed to discharge 1 mol of various products was determined. The results were:

	copper	iodine	silver	chlorine	hydrogen	tin	lead
anode	—	1	—	1	—	—	—
cathode	2	—	1	—	1	2	2

   a Using the symbol e^- to represent an electron, write ionic equations to represent all the discharges.
   b Write formulae for hydrogen chloride, silver(I) iodide, copper iodide, and lead(II) chloride based on the information from the electrolysis.
   c What volume of chlorine gas would be liberated when 10 F is passed through a solution of lead(II) chloride?
   d What weight of hydrogen would be liberated when 0·1 F is passed through dilute sulphuric(VI) acid solution?
   e How many Faradays would have been needed to liberate 1 mol of oxygen gas?

11.3   Quantities deposited on electrolysis

The diagram illustrates the apparatus used to investigate the weight of metal deposited on, or removed from, metal electrodes during electrolysis. After passing a constant current for 161 minutes, the anode in beaker 1 lost 0·32 g copper, the anode in beaker 2 lost 0·64 g copper, and the cathode in beaker 3 gained 1·08 g silver.
   a What weight of silver would be deposited by 1 F?
   b How many coulombs of electricity must have been passed in this experiment?
   c Calculate the current which must have flowed.
   d What weight of copper would be deposited on the cathode of beaker 1?

e Which of the following is a reasonable deduction for beaker 2?
   1 The ions in beaker 2 have twice the charge of ions in beaker 1.
   2 The ions in beaker 2 have half the charge of ions in beaker 1.
   3 Twice as many ions are liberated in beaker 2 as in beaker 1.

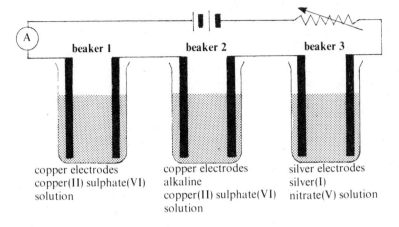

copper electrodes
copper(II) sulphate(VI)
solution

copper electrodes
alkaline
copper(II) sulphate(VI)
solution

silver electrodes
silver(I)
nitrate(V) solution

11.4   Simple cell formation

1 A simple cell is shown in the diagram.
   a Write ionic equations
      1 for the anode reaction
      2 for the cathode reaction
      3 for the overall reaction.
   b Indicate the direction of current flow and the direction of electron
      flow.
   c Which metal is the most reactive?

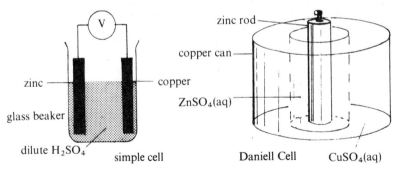

simple cell   Daniell Cell $CuSO_4$(aq)

2 The Daniell Cell (see diagram) is a more practical version of the
apparatus in question 1. What is its e.m.f? Why is it better?
The reaction of zinc with dilute sulphuric(VI) acid is rather slow. Adding
copper turnings, or copper(II) sulphate(VI) speeds it up. Explain this in
the light of what you know about simple cells.

11.5 Electrochemical series

1 Consider the elements calcium, iron, zinc and magnesium with regard to their ability to
  a displace one another from their salts
  b react with water, steam and hydrochloric acid.
Place the four elements in a series to conform with their reactivity. What is the series called?

2 Name:
  a a metal which burns easily in air
  b a metal which would displace copper from copper(II) sulphate(VI) solution
  c a metal which will **not** react with a dilute acid
  d a metal which will **not** react with concentrated nitric(V) acid.

11.6 Simple cell formation and corrosion

The diagram represents a pit in a metal-plated, metal sheet.

  a If the electrode potential of Zn is $-0.74\,V$, and of Fe, $-0.44\,V$, which metal will dissolve the quicker when the pit fills with water?
  b Which will corrode the quicker, tinned mild steel or galvanised steel sheets? Write an explanation.
  c One modern method of avoiding corrosion is to spray and coat with plastic. How does this prevent corrosion?
  d Pipeline operators use magnesium rods set into the pipeline at intervals to stop corrosion. Why are they effective?
  e Some commercial rust removers and protectors consist of a strong solution of phosphoric(V) acid. Why are they effective?

Objective test 11

Questions 1–5   Apply Rubric A instructions

1 Which of the following will conduct the largest current through a standard voltameter using a standard e.m.f. source?
  A 0.1M NaOH   D 1M ammonia
  B 1M NaOH   E distilled water
  C 2M sugar solution

2 Which will require the expenditure of the greatest amount of current for the liberation of 1 mol of product?

    A making aluminium by the electrolysis of molten, dissolved cryolite
    B making sodium by the electrolysis of molten rock salt
    C making oxygen by the electrolysis of acidified water
    D making chlorine by the electrolysis of brine
    E making hydrogen by the electrolysis of dilute sodium hydroxide

3 Which of the following is the quantity of electricity passed through a voltameter when the current is 1·5 amps and it is passed for 128 minutes?

    A 0·75 F   B 1·20 F   C 7·5 F   D 12·0 F   E 0·120 F

4 In which simple cell will the first named metal corrode first?

    A copper/zinc   D silver/iron
    B iron/tin   E silver/copper
    C copper/iron

5 Which of the following arrangements give the largest current with a voltameter containing 1 M HCl?

    A 6 V battery, 1 cm^2 platinum electrodes—10 cm apart
    B 12 V battery, 1 cm^2 platinum electrodes— 5 cm apart
    C 6 V battery, 4 cm^2 platinum electrodes— 5 cm apart
    D 6 V battery, 4 cm^2 platinum electrodes—20 cm apart
    E 12 V battery, 2 cm^2 platinum electrodes—10 cm apart

Questions 6–14   Apply Rubric B instructions

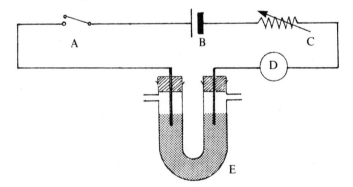

Which of the components A, B, C, D and E is used to

6 vary the current during an electrolysis?

7 switch off the current?

8 measure the rate of current flow?

9 change the e.m.f. across the electrodes?

10 segregate the products of electrolysis?

The following are ionic equations for electrode reactions

A $2H^+ + 2e^- \longrightarrow H_2$ D $4OH^- \longrightarrow 2H_2O + O_2 + 4e^-$
B $2Cl^- \longrightarrow Cl_2 + 2e^-$ E $2O^{2-} \longrightarrow O_2 + 4e^-$
C $Cu - 2e^- \longrightarrow Cu^{2+}$

11 Which equation does not usually apply to aqueous solutions?

12 Which are the reactions which take place in the water voltameter?

13 Which equation(s) represent the electrolytic decomposition of brine?

14 Which equation represents an anode dissolving?

Questions 15–20   Apply Rubric C instructions

15 An electrolyte is
  1 a covalent substance of low melting point
  2 a highly conducting metal
  3 any compound soluble in water
  4 an ionic substance.

16 Cations are formed
  1 when a metal gains protons
  2 when a metal loses protons
  3 when a metal gains electrons
  4 when a metal loses electrons.

17 A Faraday is
  1 96 500 coulombs
  2 the amount of current needed to liberate 1 mol of substance
  3 1 mol of electrons
  4 volts × amps × time in seconds.

18 In the electrolysis of copper(II) sulphate(VI) using platinum electrodes
  1 the solution gradually becomes colourless
  2 copper deposits at the cathode
  3 sulphuric(VI) acid forms around the anode
  4 hydrogen is liberated at the anode.

19 Ions are
  1 always neutralised by gain of electrons
  2 charged particles having more electrons than protons
  3 always neutralised by loss of electrons
  4 charged particles with an unbalanced number of protons and electrons.

20 Electrode potentials measure
  1 the relative reactivities of two metals dissolving in common solutions
  2 the relative abilities of two metals to lose electrons and form ions
  3 the relative abilities of two metal ions to gain electrons and form the metal
  4 the potential difference which exists between two metals when they are immersed in a conducting solution.

Chapter 12   Oxidation and reduction

1 Define oxidation
   a with reference to oxygen and hydrogen
   b with reference to electrons.
   c Give one example to illustrate each type.
   d The following are oxidising agents:
     oxygen, manganese(IV) oxide, potassium manganate(VII), sodium
     chlorate(I).
     Describe one reaction involving each in turn by writing equations.
   e Using arrows, or any other device of your choosing, indicate why
     you regard the effect as oxidation.

2 Explain the following observations in terms of oxidation or reduction.
   a When a lump of lead is left in silver(I) nitrate(V) solution 'trees' of
     crystalline silver grow out from the lead lump.
   b When hydrogen sulphide gas is burned at a jet, in contact with the
     underside of a cool beaker, sulphur is deposited on the beaker.
   c When sulphur dioxide is bubbled into orange potassium chromate
     (VI) solution it turns green.
   d When black copper(II) oxide is heated vigorously with charcoal
     powder a brown powder is left.
   e Heating a mixture of magnesium powder with litharge produces
     beads of a metal which will mark paper.

3 In the following reactions which *reactants* are reductants and which
oxidants?
   a $HgO + H_2 \longrightarrow Hg + H_2O$
   b $Br_2 + 2I^-(aq) \longrightarrow 2Br^-(aq) + I_2$
   c $Cu^{2+}(aq) + Mg \longrightarrow Mg^{2+} + Cu$
   d $C + H_2O(g) \longrightarrow CO + H_2$
   e $Fe_2O_3 + 3CO \longrightarrow 2Fe + 3CO_2$

4 The order of reactivity of five divalent metals is A, B, C, D and E, such
that A is the most reactive.
   a Which is the most powerful reducing agent?
   b 1 mol A reacted with water to give 1 mol hydrogen. Write an equation
     and indicate which reactant is the oxidant.
   c Which metal would you expect to be most easily prepared by
     reduction of its ores with carbon?
   d Which metal will not displace any of the others from solutions of their
     salts?
   e Given solutions of salts of each metal describe how you would show
     that the order given is correct.

Objective test 12

Questions 1–2   Apply Rubric A instructions

1 Which reactant (underlined) is not an oxidant?

A $2H_2S + \underline{O_2} \longrightarrow 2H_2O + 2S$

B $\underline{MnO_2} + 4HCl \longrightarrow MnCl_2 + 2H_2O + Cl_2$

C $2H_2S + \underline{SO_2} \longrightarrow 2H_2O + 3S$

D $C_2H_4 + \underline{2Cl_2} \longrightarrow 2C + 4HCl$

E $CuO + \underline{CO} \longrightarrow Cu + CO_2$

2 Which of the following ionic equations involves oxidation?

A $Fe^{3+} + e^- \longrightarrow Fe^{2+}$

B $Na^+ + e^- \longrightarrow Na$

C $Cl_2 + 2e^- \longrightarrow 2Cl^-$

D $2H^+ + 2e^- \longrightarrow H_2$

E $2O^{2-} - 4e^- \longrightarrow O_2$

Questions 3–7   Apply Rubric B instructions

The following are reductants

A aluminium

B carbon

C carbon monoxide

D sodium

E iodide ions

Indicate which

3 is gaseous

4 are commonly used to reduce metal ores

5 is used to produce molten iron in the Thermit reaction

6 become oxides

7 are normally used in aqueous solutions.

Questions 8–10   Apply Rubric C instructions

8 The first aluminium was made by reacting the oxide with sodium. The reason for this was that

1 sodium is more reactive than aluminium

2 aluminium cannot be made by reduction with charcoal

3 sodium is more easily made by electrolysis than aluminium

4 the melting point of aluminium is very high.

9 Zinc is a more powerful reductant than copper because
1 zinc will become coated with copper in copper(II) sulphate(VI) solution
2 zinc becomes tarnished much more rapidly in moist air
3 copper is found native and zinc is not
4 copper loses electrons more easily than zinc.

10 If the order of reactivity of three **non**-metals is $X > Y > Z$ then
1 Z is the more powerful oxidising agent
2 X will displace Z from a solution of its salts
3 Z will react the most vigorously with hydrogen
4 Y will displace Z from a solution of its salts.

SECTION THREE
CHEMICALS
AND THE ENVIRONMENT

Chapter 13   Chemicals and air

13.1   Composition of air

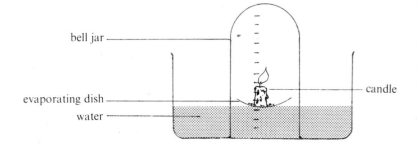

1 The apparatus shown was used to determine the volume composition
of air. Before the candle was lit the levels of water inside and outside the
bell jar were equalised.
Account for the following observations:
  a As burning commenced the level of water in the bell jar went down.
  b After a few minutes the candle went out.
  c The level of water started to creep up **slowly** after this.
  d The level finally settled at a point indicating about 10% oxygen.
  e What would be the advantage of using phosphorus instead of a
  candle?

2 Account for the following sequential observations.
  a A large volume of air was compressed to a very small volume. It
  became hot.
  b The compressed air was left at room temperature. It cooled to the
  same temperature as the surroundings.
  c The compressed air was allowed to escape into a container of large
  volume. The temperature of the container dropped well below room
  temperature.
  d Successive operations of type **a, b** and **c** led to the formation of a
  liquid at a temperature of $-200°C$.
  e When the liquid was warmed to $-196°C$ an inert gas was given off
  and $\frac{4}{5}$ths of the volume of liquid changed to this gas.
  f The remainder only changed to a gas at $-183°C$.

3 The apparatus shown was operated.

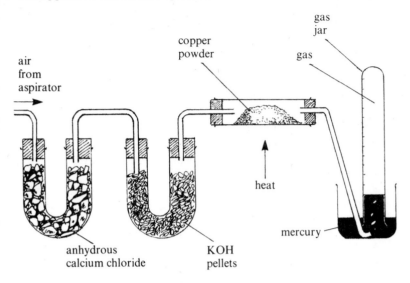

a What is the gas collected in the gas jar?
b What gas does the KOH remove?
c What happens to the copper powder?
d The weight of copper increased 0·16 g. What volume of gas would be collected?
e Assuming that the air was 1% moist what would be the increase in weight of the calcium chloride tube?

13.2 Oxygen

1 a Which of the following reactions is the most convenient for obtaining a controlled supply of oxygen?

(i) $2MnO_2(s)\xrightarrow[\text{high temp}]{\text{heat}}2MnO + O_2$

(ii) $2H_2O_2(l)\xrightarrow[\text{KMnO}_4\text{ solution}]{\text{saturated}}2H_2O + O_2$

(iii) $2H_2O_2(l)\xrightarrow[\text{catalyst}]{\text{MnO}_2}2H_2O + O_2$

(iv) $2KClO_3(s)\xrightarrow[\text{catalyst}]{\text{MnO}_2}2KCl + 3O_2$

b List the advantages and disadvantages of each method.
c Draw a diagram of a suitable apparatus for the method chosen.
d If the oxygen were required dry what modifications would have to be made to the apparatus?

2 Indicate what you would see happening and the nature of the product when deflagrating spoons containing the following are plunged into gas jars of oxygen.

    a burning sulphur   **d** glowing splint

    b dry phosphorus   **e** heated calcium

    c heated steel wool

What colour would result if the contents of the gas jars were shaken with water containing a little universal indicator?

3 Account for the following:

    a Inhaled air turned anhydrous copper(II) sulphate(VI) blue more slowly than exhaled air.

    b Exhaled air turned limewater milky more quickly after the pupil had stepped on and off a chair thirty times.

    c If a beaker of inflammable liquid catches fire it may be put out by covering with an asbestos sheet.

    d Water containing decomposing sewage does not support life.

    e Heart patients may sometimes be put in an oxygen tent.

    f A whiff of carbon dioxide is sometimes given when breathing seems to have stopped.

    g When fruit is bottled, or food put in the deep freeze, precautions are taken to exclude air.

13.3 Oxides and their classification

1 Describe how you would prepare a reasonably pure sample of each of the following oxides starting from the *element*.

    a magnesium oxide   **d** phosphorus(V) oxide

    b copper(II) oxide   **e** water

    c carbon monoxide

2 Give an example in each case and write an equation.

    a An alkaline oxide reacting with water to form an alkali.

    b An alkaline oxide reacting with a neutral oxide to form a solid salt.

    c A basic oxide reacting with an acid to form a salt and water.

    d A basic oxide reacting with an acid oxide to form a salt.

    e An acidic oxide reacting with water to form an acid.

3 Identify the type of oxide concerned in each of the following cases and write equations for any reactions.

    a X_2O_3, insoluble and amphoteric.

    b X_4O_{10}, violent reaction with water. Fumes in moist air.

    c $(XO_2)_n$, white, crystalline, insoluble. Dissolves slowly in strong alkali.

    d XO, yellow powder, turns brown when heated in oxygen.

    e X_2O_2, white powder, does not give oxygen on heating.

    f X_3O_4, brilliant red powder. Used in paints.

    g X_2O, colourless gas with anaesthetic qualities.

    h XO_2, brown powder which gives oxygen on heating and leaves a yellow oxide.

13.4 Hydrogen peroxide

1 All the following relate to the preparation of hydrogen peroxide. Explain the parts of the description which are underlined.

A solution of dilute sulphuric(VI) acid is cooled to 0°C in a distilling flask. An excess of barium peroxide is added taking care to keep the temperature constant. The solution is filtered. The aqueous solution obtained is distilled under reduced pressure. The initial distillate boiling at 100°C is discarded. The portion left boils at approximately 150°C. It is stored in a dark brown bottle.

2 What is meant by the term '20 volume' H_2O_2?
A solution of H_2O_2 was decomposed to oxygen by adding a suitable catalyst. 10 cm^3 of the solution produced 150 cm^3 of oxygen at s.t.p.
  a What is the volume strength of the H_2O_2?
  b What mol of oxygen is produced per mol of H_2O_2 according to an equation?
  c Determine the mol of H_2O_2 in the original 10 cm^3.
  d What is the molarity of the hydrogen peroxide solution?
  e What would be the molarity of '20 volume' H_2O_2?

13.5 Nitrogen

1 a Describe how you would prepare a sample of comparatively pure nitrogen from laboratory air.
  b Describe how you might prepare nitrogen in the laboratory from laboratory chemicals.
  c In what way would the two samples of nitrogen differ?
  d What is the reaction of nitrogen with fiercely burning magnesium? Write an equation and indicate what happens when the product is dissolved in water.
  e Nitrogen will react with oxygen in an electrical discharge. What are the major sources of electrical discharges in cities? Name the product of the reaction.

2 In 1894, Lord Rayleigh prepared nitrogen by passing air mixed with an excess of ammonia over heated copper. The ammonia reacted with oxygen forming nitrogen and water. The gas was dried and its density found. Another sample of nitrogen was made by passing air over heated copper. The density was found. Finally, nitrogen was made by passing oxygen and ammonia over heated copper. The density of the dried nitrogen was again found.
  a None of the gases had the **same** density. Why not?
  b Which 'nitrogen' could be expected to have the lower density? Explain your reasoning.
  c Which gas would be expected to contain the most contaminants?
  d Identify three of the contaminants.

3 a Draw a version of the nitrogen cycle.

b Draw up two columns headed *sources of nitrogenous fertilisers* and *origins of nitrogenous losses*. Try to list as many as possible sources and origins.

c What place do beans have in the principle of crop rotation?

d Why are nitrates(V) fed to plants harmless, but nitrates(V) in drinking water harmful?

13.6 Ammonia

1 The laboratory preparation of ammonia can be difficult unless precautions are taken. The following mistakes are often made. Explain why they are mistakes.

a A solution of sodium hydroxide is used instead of flaked sodium hydroxide or soda-lime.

b Incomplete mixing of sodium hydroxide and ammonium chloride is achieved, or a large excess of ammonium chloride is used.

c Calcium chloride may be used for drying instead of calcium oxide.

d The gas jars used for collecting the gas may be wet, or the calcium oxide may not have been freshly dried.

e The gas may be collected by downward delivery.

Now draw the ideal apparatus and appropriately label it. Write an equation for the reaction.

2 Industrially, ammonia is made by the Haber process.

a Write an equation to represent the equilibrium of ammonia formation from hydrogen and nitrogen.

b The conditions call for high pressure and a catalyst. Explain why these are necessary.

c An optimum temperature of 550°C is called for. Considering the reaction is exothermic why is such a high temperature necessary?

d Hydrogen can be obtained by 'cracking' petroleum oil. What is meant by the term 'cracking'?

e The ammonia formed during each cycle is removed as liquid. What conditions are necessary to liquefy a gas like ammonia?

3 a Ammonia is an alkaline gas. What does this mean?

b The concentration of ammonium ions in aqueous solution never rises above $1\cdot8 \times 10^{-5}$ mol dm^{-3}. Is ammonia a strong or weak alkali?

c The normal ammonia sold to laboratories contains over 1000 cm^3 of ammonia dissolved per dm^3. Why is ammonia so soluble in water? (Same reason that water has a high mp!)

d The ammonia molecule has a pyramidal shape. Why is it not trigonal planar?

e Ammonia forms coordinate covalent bonds. Explain how this happens when ammonia reacts with hydrogen chloride gas.

13.7 Nitric(V) acid

1 A pupil carrying out the preparation and testing of nitric(V) acid used the following procedures. Explain the reasons for the procedures underlined.

  a She used an all-glass apparatus and avoided rubber tubing.
  b She heated a mixture of sodium nitrate(V) and concentrated sulphuric(VI) acid on a sand bath.
  c The brown fumes given off were condensed.
  d The residual liquid in the distilling flask was poured away carefully into a sink with the taps running.
  e The nitric(V) acid caused the ignition of dry, warm, sawdust.

2 Describe how ammonia is converted to nitric(V) acid and to nitrates(V). Specifically

  a write an equation for the overall reaction
  b write equations for each step in the process
  c indicate the conditions of temperature, catalyst and intermediate temperatures.
  d Why is the process so important?
  e What was the principle source of nitrates(V) prior to the Haber process?

3 When a spark plug is inserted in a bottle of air (see diagram) and connected to a working induction coil, a brown gas is produced.

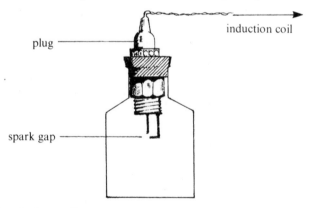

induction coil

plug

spark gap

  a What is the gas?
  b The brown gas was used as a catalyst in a process for converting SO_2 to SO_3. What will be the consequences of the release of SO_2 together with the brown gas in the exhaust fumes of a car?
  c Under what conditions may the brown gas harm parts of the motor vehicle?
  d Electrical discharge methods were once used to prepare nitric(V) acid from air. Why has the method been discontinued?

13.8 Carbon dioxide

1 The diagram represents a means of preparing a steady stream of dry carbon dioxide. Indicate four reasons why this method is unsatisfactory.

Re-draw the diagram correcting all the faults and give an equation for the reaction.

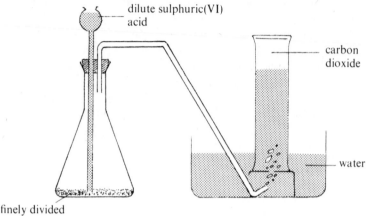

2 Explain the similarity between the burning of a wooden splint and respiration.

If breath is exhaled through limewater, describe what you would see and explain what has happened.

13.9 Carbon monoxide

1 During an air raid in the winter of 1941 a group of people sheltering in an unventilated shelter tried to keep themselves warm with a coke fire. The following morning they were all found to be dead. One peculiar feature was that they all had rosy complexions. Explain fully what had occurred.

2 Draw up a table to compare the properties of carbon dioxide and carbon monoxide.

If the formula of carbon dioxide is known to be CO_2, how would you show the formula of carbon monoxide to be CO?

Objective test 13

Questions 1–4   Apply Rubric A instructions

1 Which of the following gases is **not** present in air?
   A O_2 B Ar   C CO_2 D H_2 E N_2

2 Which of the following oxides is correctly named nitrogen(IV) oxide?
   A NO   B N_2O C NO_2 D N_2O_3 E N_2O_5

3 Which of the following is **not** true of ammonia?
   A It burns in oxygen.   D It forms white fumes with hydrogen
   B It is a very soluble gas.   chloride gas.
   C It is a strong alkali.   E It turns red litmus paper blue.

4 Which of the following does **not** apply to nitrogen?
   A It is an inert gas.
   B Under suitable conditions it forms an alkaline hydride.
   C It will react with magnesium at high temperature.
   D It is manufactured by fractional distillation of liquid air.
   E It is more soluble in water than oxygen.

Questions 5–33   Apply Rubric B instructions

Questions 5–9 refer to the chemicals

   A hydrogen chloride   D copper(II) sulphate(VI)
   B copper(II) oxide   E iron(III) oxide
   C oxygen

5 The chemical gives a dense white cloud with ammonia.

6 The chemical gives a deep blue solution with ammonia.

7 The chemical may be reduced by ammonia.

8 The chemicals oxidise ammonia.

9 The chemical catalyses the preparation of ammonia.

Questions 10–14 refer to the following types of oxides:

   A amphoteric oxide   D alkaline oxide
   B acidic oxide   E basic oxide
   C neutral oxide

10 A white oxide, insoluble in water but gives a salt with dilute acid.

11 An oxide which was a colourless gas insoluble in water.

12 A white solid which turns damp litmus paper red.

13 A soluble oxide which gave ammonia when boiled with ammonium chloride.

14 The oxide dissolved in acid and in alkali.

Questions 15–19 refer to hydrogen peroxide.

Hydrogen peroxide may react

A as a reductant
B as an oxidant
C being decomposed by a catalyst

D as a bleaching agent
E causing a precipitate

Indicate which is the case in the following reactions:

15 $2H^+ + H_2O_2 + 2I^- \longrightarrow 2H_2O + I_2$

16 $2Ag(NH_3)_2^+ + H_2O_2 \longrightarrow 2Ag + O_2 + 4NH_4^+$

17 $PbS + 4H_2O_2 \longrightarrow PbSO_4 + 4H_2O$

18 $2H_2O_2 + MnO_2 \longrightarrow 2H_2O + O_2 + MnO_2$

19 $2Fe^{2+} + 2H^+ + H_2O_2 \longrightarrow 2H_2O + 2Fe^{3+}$

Questions 20–24 refer to nitrogen compounds.

The following chemicals are applied as fertilising sources of nitrogen:

A nitrate(V) of potash (KNO_3)
B nitrate(V) of soda ($NaNO_3$)
C urea $CO(NH_2)_2$
D nitro-chalk 50/50 $NH_4NO_3/CaCO_3$
E sulphate(VI) of ammonia ($(NH_4)_2SO_4$)

20 Which contains the highest fraction of nitrogen per mole?

21 Which is often of natural origin?

22 Which contains another element, apart from nitrogen, which is important for plant growth?

23 Which would cause the least amount of soil acidity?

24 Which would cause the most amount of soil acidity?

Questions 25–28 refer to the nitrogen cycle.

Nitrogen may be added to the soil as follows:

A fixed by nitrate(V) producing legumes
B the Haber process of fixation—usually added as ammonium sulphate(VI)
C the oxidation of manufactured ammonia—added as nitrates(V)
D fixed by atmospheric electrical discharges
E added as compost and manure.

Which:

25 are well suited to crop rotation?

88

26 are most important for intensive farming?

27 is likely to enhance the moisture retaining qualities of soil?

28 are natural processes?

Questions 29–33 refer to nitric(V) acid.

Nitric(V) acid will react under a variety of conditions to give
    A $NO(g)$ B $NO_2(g)$ C $NH_3(g)$ D $NO_2(g) + O_2(g)$ E $H_2(g)$
Fit the products to the conditions:

29 Poured down a red hot silica tube.

30 Very dilute acid added to magnesium.

31 Dilute acid added to an alkaline solution of aluminium and boiled.

32 50% acid added to copper.

33 Concentrated acid added to zinc.

Questions 34–37   *Apply Rubric C instructions*

34 Which of the following are true of all nitrates(V)?
   1 All nitrates(V) are soluble in water.
   2 All nitrates(V) decompose when heated to give NO_2.
   3 All nitrates(V) give brown fumes when heated with concentrated sulphuric(VI) acid.
   4 All nitrates(V) are oxidising agents.

35 Which of the following are true of all nitrates(III)?
   1 They react with dilute HCl to give brown fumes of NO_2.
   2 They are anhydrides of nitric(III) acid.
   3 They decolourise potassium manganate(VII).
   4 When heated they produce oxygen.

36 Which of the following will produce acidic oxides?
   1 sodium   2 sulphur   3 iron   4 phosphorus

37 Which of the following apply to the equilibrium reaction between hydrogen and nitrogen?
   1 It is 100% to the left at s.t.p.
   2 It is 100% to the left at very high temperatures.
   3 It is 15% to the right at 200 atmospheres and 500°C.
   4 It is 88% to the right at 200 atmospheres and 800°C.

Chapter 14   Water

14.1   Properties of water

Explain the following anomalous characteristics of water:
- **a** It has a maximum density at 4°C.
- **b** It is not a linear molecule.
- **c** It expands when it forms a solid.
- **d** It can act as a proton donor or a proton acceptor.
- **e** It is an excellent solvent for ionic compounds.

14.2   The volume composition of water

Answer the following:
- **a** How would you test to identify a liquid as water?
- **b** How would you show that water is a compound?
- **c** Describe how you would use a voltameter to determine the volume composition of water.
- **d** Explain why water is a poor conductor of electricity but many people are electrocuted in wet conditions.
- **e** Describe how you would simply show that water is a dipolar compound.

14.3   Measurement of solubility

1 Describe how you would find:
- **a** How much sodium chloride dissolved in 100 cm^3 water at 20°C.
- **b** The amount of suspended solids in a sample of muddy river water.
- **c** The percentage of dissolved solids in sea water.
- **d** The amount of heat needed to change 1 mol of liquid water to steam at 100°C.
- **e** The presence of a chloride ion (or chlorine) in tap water.

2 An anhydrous salt, of molecular weight 120, was dissolved in water and crystallised. The following results were recorded:

$$\text{weight of anhydrous salt} \quad 1{\cdot}20 \text{ g}$$
$$\text{weight of dry crystals} \quad\quad 2{\cdot}46 \text{ g}$$

- **a** How much water (g) is combined with 1·20 g of the anhydrous salt?
- **b** How much water (g) is combined with 1 mol anhydrous salt?
- **c** The crystals gave a white precipitate with barium chloride solution. Write a formula for the salt and deduce the probable atomic mass for the metal ion.
- **d** What other information would help to verify that this is the true atomic mass?

Objective test 14

Questions 1–4   Apply Rubric A instructions

1 Which of the following is insoluble in water?
   A $NaNO_3$ B $CaSO_4$ C $MgSO_4$ D Na_2CO_3 E $FeCl_2$

2 Which of the following will **not** react with water or steam even at high temperatures?
   A Mg   B Na   C Cu   D Zn   E Fe

3 Which of the following is **untrue**?
   A The weight composition of water is 11·11% hydrogen and 88·89% oxygen.
   B The volume composition of water is 2 of hydrogen to 1 of oxygen.
   C The mol ratio for water is 2 mol hydrogen to 1 mol oxygen.
   D The mol ratio for water is 1 mol hydrogen to 0·5 mol oxygen.
   E The weight ratio of hydrogen to oxygen is 1 : 16 for water.

4 Which of the following is **untrue** for solubility?
   A Solubility increases with increase in temperature.
   B The amount dissolved increases as the volume of solvent increases.
   C The solubility is decreased when evaporation takes place.
   D Pressure has hardly any effect on solubility.
   E Different chemicals have different solubilities.

Questions 5–14   Apply Rubric B instructions

The following terms all apply to substances which change when exposed to air:
   A efflorescent   D adsorbent
   B deliquescent   E absorbent
   C hygroscopic
Select the correct term.

5 A salt which becomes moist on the surface only.

6 A solid substance which turns into a solution.

7 A crystalline substance which becomes powdery by losing water.

8 A substance which takes up water by capillary action.

9 A substance which does not become moist but effectively removes traces of moisture.

Water may act as

    A a proton donor   D a hydrolysing agent

    B a proton acceptor   E an oxidant

    C a solvent

Select the correct term.

10 $HCl + H_2O \rightleftharpoons H_3O^+ + Cl^-$

11 $Na^+Cl^- + H_2O \rightleftharpoons Na^+(aq) + Cl^-(aq)$

12 $NH_3 + H_2O \rightleftharpoons NH_4^+ + OH^-$

13 $C + H_2O \rightleftharpoons CO + H_2$

14 $PCl_5 + H_2O \longrightarrow POCl_3 + 2HCl$

Questions 15–18   Apply Rubric C instructions

15 Which of the following elements are extracted from sea water?

    1 bromine   2 gold   3 magnesium   4 sodium

16 Which of the following elements leave a clear solution after reacting with water?

    1 potassium   2 sodium   3 lithium   4 calcium

17 Which of the following are true about water/water vapour equilibrium?

    1 Air will hold more moisture on a cold day than a hot day.

    2 More moisture will be lost through sweating when the humidity is low.

    3 Dew falls because the air holds more moisture at night.

    4 A fog consists of minute drops of water and is not a gas.

18 Which is true of water?

    1 Its density is a maximum of 1 g cm^3 at 277 K.

    2 It is a dipolar covalent compound.

    3 Its specific heat is higher than the specific heat of metals.

    4 It dissolves most covalent solids.

Chapter 15 Fuels

15.1 Carbon

  a Explain the term *allotropes.*
  b Draw diagrams to represent two allotropes of carbon.
  c Write down a list of the contrasting physical properties of the allotropes of carbon.
  d Explain how a variation of one allotrope, charcoal, is made.
  e Write about the uses of two allotropes of carbon, and of charcoal.

15.2 Coal

1 Explain the following observations.
  a When coal burns it often oozes a black liquid and hisses as little jets of gas escape and burn.
  b A red ash is often left behind following the combustion of coal.
  c Smokeless coal is more difficult to ignite than normal coal. When ignited it burns with a blue tinged flame and little smoke.
  d The amount of smoke produced by burning coal can be reduced by supplying more air.
  e Burning wood which is damp quickly leads to calling in the chimney sweep!

2 The diagram shows a simplified flow-sheet of coal gas production.

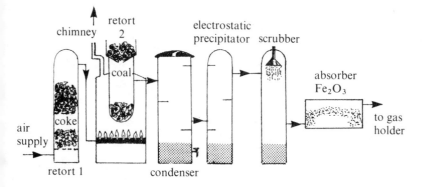

  a What fuel gas is formed in the first retort?
  b Why is the coal in the second retort heated externally?
  c What is the function of the condenser and electrostatic precipitator?
  d Water sprays from the top of the scrubber. Why is this?
  e The absorbers are to remove H_2S. Why is it removed and what reaction is involved? Write an equation.
  f Sulphur may be recovered from so-called 'spent' oxide by exposing it to the air. Write an equation for this reaction.

15.3 Petroleum and the properties of alkanes

1 Explain the following terms by writing brief notes.
   a The *fractional distillation* of petroleum oil.
   b The *catalytic cracking* of gas oil.
   c The *destructive distillation* of coal.
   d *Water gas* and *producer gas*.
   e A *saturated* hydrocarbon.

2 Explain the following observations.
   a When a jar of chlorine was inverted over a candle it went out.
   b When chlorine and North Sea gas are mixed and exposed to ultra-violet light the gaseous products do not bleach litmus paper.
   c When black viscous crude oil is fractionally distilled a colourless liquid appears in the collecting flask initially.
   d After an oil was 'cracked' the viscosity increased drastically.

15.4 Cracking

The diagram shows how ethene may be made in the classroom.

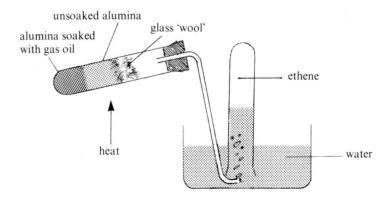

a The unsoaked alumina is heated first rather than that which is soaked. Why?
b An oily layer floats on the surface of the water following the experiment. What is it?
c Describe what you would see if the fumes given off were directly burned.
d What is the function of the alumina?
e What would be the action of the gas collected on bromine water?

Objective test 15

Questions 1–5   Apply Rubric A instructions

1 Which of the following is a property of both graphite and diamond?
  A good electrical conductance   D good lubricating properties
  B high refractive index   E extreme hardness
  C burning to carbon dioxide

2 Which is **not** true of allotropes?
  A They have different crystalline forms.
  B The spatial arrangement of their atoms is different.
  C They melt at different melting points.
  D They have different physical properties.
  E They have different chemical properties.

3 Which of the fuels has the highest % carbon?
  A anthracite   B lignite   C peat   D paraffin   E methane

4 Which of the following is **not** a product of combustion of fuels?
  A carbon monoxide   D carbon
  B water   E hydrogen
  C carbon dioxide

5 Which of the following is not an alkane?
  A CH_4 B C_8H_{18} C C_2H_4 D C_3H_8 E C_5H_{12}

Questions 6–16   Apply Rubric B instructions

The following are fuels
  A CO   B CH_4 C carbon   D H_2 E C_4H_{10}

6 Which requires the most O_2 per mol of fuel burned?

7 Which requires the most O_2 per kg of fuel burned?

8 Which do not produce steam as a by-product?

9 Which fuel gives the most heat per unit mass?

10 Which fuel is usually stored in steel 'bottles' and used by campers?

11 Which fuel is the most difficult to ignite and store?

Coke may be used

   A as a fuel

   B as a source of more convenient fuels

   C as a source of synthesis gas for the Haber process

   D as a reducing agent in metal production

   E as a material in ethyne production.

Which of the above is involved in the following processes?

12 A carefully controlled mixture of air and steam is passed through white-hot coke.

13 The coke is burned in an excess of air.

14 The coke is heated with limestone in an electric furnace and the product treated with water.

15 The coke is heated with cerussite at high temperature. The high temperature is produced by passing in very hot air.

16 Steam is passed over hot coke with some air. The gases are passed with more steam over an iron catalyst. CO_2 is removed under pressure through water.

Questions 17–19   Apply Rubric C instructions

17 It has been shown that lignite, a cheap and abundant brown coal, is excellent for desert reclamation. Which of the following factors contribute?

   1 The lignite breaks down in hot conditions more slowly than normal organic matter.

   2 Lignite can absorb and retain large quantities of water.

   3 Lignite contains a large amount of compressed organic matter.

   4 Lignite reflects some of the sun's heat.

18 Gas may be made by anaerobic decomposition of domestic refuse. Which of the following are likely products?

   1 CH_4 2 NH_3 3 H_2S 4 SO_2

19 An alkene

   1 is an unsaturated hydrocarbon

   2 burns with a bright blue flame

   3 has the general formula C_2H_{2n}

   4 is less reactive than alkanes.

Chapter 16   Chemicals from oil

16.1   Properties of alkenes

1 The following is a simplified flow-sheet of a refinery process.

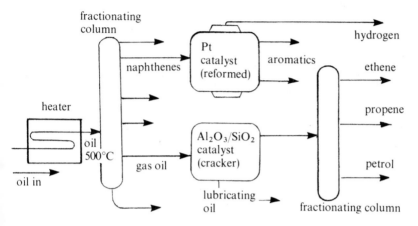

a What are the main products of the fractionating column?
b Why is the incoming oil heated to 500°C?
c The gas oil fraction is fed into a cracker. What is the purpose of this?
d At which point in the process are alkenes formed?
e In what ways are the alkenes utilised?

2 a Write out, in two columns, the differences in properties between alkanes and alkenes paying special attention to (i) their combustion (ii) their action with bromine (iii) their action with potassium manganate(VII) (iv) their action with hydrogen.
  b Draw up a list of some possible by-products of ethene and propene.
  c Write a simple equation to illustrate the polymerisation of ethene.
  d How is polythene usually made?
  e How is ethane-1,2-diol made and what uses does it have? Write out its formula.

3 a Draw diagrams to show the structural formulae of (i) ethane (ii) ethene (iii) ethyne.
  b Under what conditions does ethene react with (i) hydrogen (ii) hydrogen chloride? In each case, write an equation and name the product.
  c Under what conditions does ethyne react with an excess of (i) hydrogen (ii) bromine? In each case write an equation and name the product.
  d When ethyne reacts with hydrogen chloride, a compound is formed which will undergo polymerisation. Draw a diagram to illustrate the structure of a section of the polymer which is formed.

16.2 Industrial chemicals from alkenes

1 a What are isomers?
 b Write the structural formulae and name the isomers of C_4H_{10}.
 c Explain the meaning of the statement *'polythene is a polymer'*.
 d Name the chemical processes, and explain briefly what happens, when polythene is made from petroleum oil.
 e What is the chief chemical characteristic of polythene which makes it useful?
 f Why is the heavy organic chemical industry situated near the coast?

2 Answer the following by writing a few lines in each case.
 a Why are the Americans turning to the cracking of fuel oil for a source of domestic gas?
 b Why has the UK discontinued making gas from coal?
 c Why is natural gas transported in refrigerated ships?
 d There has been a suggestion that natural gas be converted to methanol and transported in that way. What might be the advantages?
 e Would you think that methanol is a better fuel than natural gas?
 f Why are the various units of refinery and petrochemical complexes built so close together?

Objective test 16

Questions 1–4   Apply Rubric A instructions

1 To which of the following may the term unsaturated be applied?
 A C_2H_4 B CH_4 C C_3H_8 D C_4H_{10} E C_7H_{16}

2 Which of the following structural formulae represents an alkyne?
 A $H_2C{=}CH_2$ D $CH_3{-}C{\equiv}CH$
 B $H_3C{-}CH_3$ E $CH_3{-}CH_2{-}CH_3$
 C $CH_3{-}CH{=}CH_2$

3 Which of the following is true of an alkane?
 A It reacts with bromine.
 B It decolourises potassium manganate(VII).
 C It burns with a smoky flame.
 D It reacts with hydrogen.
 E It reacts with chlorine in ultra violet light.

4 Which of the following is the formula of 2-methylpropene?
 A $CH_3CH_2CH_3$ D $CH_3CH{=}CH_2$
 B $CH_3C{\equiv}CH_2$ E $CH_3CH{=}CHCH_3$
 C $CH_3C(CH_3){=}CH_2$

Questions 5–14   Apply Rubric B instructions

Ethene forms a series of products as follows:
  A glycol   D ethanol
  B vinyl chloride   E 1-chloro-2-hydroxyethane
  C polythene
Fit the correct product to the conditions given.

5 High pressure, 200°C.

6 High pressure, dilute sulphuric(VI) acid at 370 K.

7 Catalyst and chlorine at 500°C.

8 Aqueous potassium manganate(VII).

9 Chlorine water at room temperature.

The following are five important organic chemicals made from oil.
  A ethene   B P.V.C.   C propathene   D propene   E chloroethene

10 Which are gases at room temperature?

11 Which are polymers?

12 Which are monomers?

13 Which is used for plastic guttering and downspouts?

14 Which is used for making plastic chairs?

Questions 15–17   Apply Rubric C instructions

15 The term *addition compound* refers to
      1 a compound adding to a double bond
      2 a compound formed by elimination of a double bond
      3 a compound having hydrogen added to it
      4 a compound possessing double or treble bonds which combines
        with a reactant additively to form an addition compound.

16 The following is true of polymers.
      1 They have a very high molecular weight.
      2 They are indestructible by burning.
      3 They consist of simple units repeated many times.
      4 They can **all** be melted and reformed many times.

17 The following chemicals can be made directly from oil:
      1 paraffin   2 methane   3 hydrogen   4 nylon

Chapter 17　Carbohydrates

17.1　Energy and carbohydrates

The equation representing photosynthesis is as follows:

$$6CO_2 + 6H_2O \rightleftharpoons C_6H_{12}O_6 + 6O_2 ; \Delta H + 2800 \text{ kJ mol}^{-1}$$

a Name the products and reactants in photosynthesis.
b The reaction is highly endothermic. Where does this considerable energy come from and how does the plant mobilise this energy?
c Describe how the reactants are taken in by the plant.
d What would be the effect of increasing the concentration of the gaseous reactant? At one period the earth's atmosphere did contain high amounts of this gas. What were the consequences?
e What conditions favour the reverse of the forward reaction above?

17.2　Glucose and the carbon cycle

1 In an experiment on photosynthesis and respiration of green plants two identical leaves were placed in sealed test-tubes with a little clear bicarbonate indicator (thymol blue in sodium hydrogen carbonate). One tube was kept in darkness and the other exposed to sunlight. A third tube contained no leaf. In the darkened tube there was a colour change from orange to yellow and in the exposed tube from orange to red.
  a What reaction must have been predominant in the test-tube kept in the dark? Explain fully why the indicator changed colour.
  b What reaction must have been predominant in the exposed tube? Again explain fully why the indicator changed colour.
  c Why was a third tube necessary?
  d Does the experiment prove that respiration ceases during photosynthesis?
  e Does the experiment prove that photosynthesis ceases during respiration?
  f Sodium hydrogen carbonate indicator is not a test for a specific acid gas but will change colour in any acid gas. What doubt does this throw on the results of the experiment?

2 The following equilibria are important in relation to the concentration of carbon dioxide in the atmosphere:

$$CO_2 + H_2O \rightleftharpoons H_2CO_3 ; C + O_2 \rightleftharpoons CO_2$$

$$6CO_2 + 6H_2O \underset{\text{plants}}{\rightleftharpoons} C_6H_{12}O_6 + 6O_2$$

$$H_2CO_3 + CaCO_3 \rightleftharpoons Ca(HCO_3)_2$$

sea

rock　　marine　　　soluble
　　　　animals

What is likely to happen in the following cases?

a If the amount of carbon dioxide builds up massively because of fuel burning.

b If the earth's surface becomes denuded of plants.

c If the sea becomes barren because of nuclear contamination.

d If the sea warms up a few degrees.

e If the concentration of oxygen in the atmosphere is drastically reduced by combustion.

17.3 Comparison of the properties of carbohydrates

The following separate tests were carried out. Indicate their results.

tests	results
a A drop of starch solution was added to iodine solution.	
b $1 cm^3$ of the same starch solution was added to saliva and left for 48 hours at 25°C. Iodine solution was added.	
c $1 cm^3$ of starch solution was boiled with Fehling's solution.	
d The solution treated as in **b** was boiled with Fehling's solution.	
e Glucose was heated with Fehling's solution.	
f Glucose was added to iodine solution.	
g Starch boiled with dilute HCl was added to Fehling's solution.	
h Starch boiled with dilute HCl was added to iodine solution.	

i What do the sequences of results demonstrate experimentally?

17.4 Formation of alcohol by fermentation

1 Explain the following underlined facts.

a Yeast is added to bread dough before baking.

b Sodium hydrogen carbonate is added to cake mixes before baking.

c Sometimes yeast is added to warmed sugar solution before being added to dough.

d Wines must be racked before storage.

e Preserves must be heated for some time at a temperature above 90°C and stored out of contact with air.

2 The apparatus shown was set up.

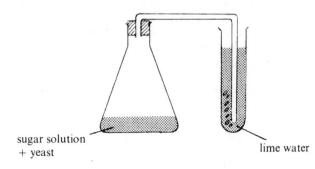

sugar solution
+ yeast

lime water

Explain the following.
  a During the first hour nothing happened that was visible.
  b After 24 hours a steady stream of bubbles was emerging and the lime water turned milky.
  c Subsequently, the number of bubbles emerging per second had slowed down. They again increased for a period when the solution was diluted slightly.
  d When the solution was distilled the first fraction collected came over between 78–84°C and caught fire when a match was applied to it.

Objective test 17

Questions 1–4   Apply Rubric A instructions

1 Which of the following is not necessary for photosynthesis?
  A sunlight   D water
  B chlorophyll   E carbon dioxide
  C oxygen

2 Which of the following would prevent fermentation?
  A low pressure   D lack of oxygen
  B low temperature   E lack of nitrogen
  C 7% alcohol

3 Which of the following is not a breaking-down process?
  A fermentation   D polymerisation
  B digestion   E hydrolysis
  C composting

4 Which of the following is not utilised in animal respiration?
  A starch   B glucose   C fat   D sucrose   E cellulose

The following are equations of some carbohydrate reactions. Fit the correct term to each reaction.

A respiration	D combustion
B digestion	E dehydration
C polymerisation	F fermentation

5 $C_6H_{12}O_6 + 6O_2 \longrightarrow 6CO_2 + 6H_2O$

6 $C_{12}H_{22}O_{11} + H_2O \xrightarrow{\text{enzymes}} C_6H_{12}O_6 + C_6H_{12}O_6$

7 $nC_6H_{12}O_6 \longrightarrow (C_6H_{10}O_5)_n + nH_2O$

8 $C_{12}H_{22}O_{11} + 12O_2 \longrightarrow 12CO_2 + 11H_2O$

9 $C_6H_{12}O_6 \xrightarrow{\text{enzymes}} 2C_2H_5OH + 2CO_2$

10 $C_{12}H_{22}O_{11} \xrightarrow[\text{H}_2\text{SO}_4]{\text{conc.}} 12C(-11H_2O)$

11 Which of the following applies to the carbon cycle?
 1 The amount of carbon dioxide in the air steadily increases.
 2 Decay converts carbon compounds to carbon dioxide and water.
 3 Plants are the only means of preventing the carbon dioxide content of the atmosphere from rising.
 4 Respiration has the same products as decay.

12 Which of the following processes do **not** require the presence of air?
 1 putrefaction
 2 composting
 3 fermenting
 4 rotting

Chapter 18   Chemicals from salt

18.1   Manufacture of sodium carbonate

1 The ammonia-soda process depends on two equilibria

$$Na^+(aq) + HCO_3^-(aq) \rightleftharpoons NaHCO_3(s)$$
$$CO_2(g) + H_2O \rightleftharpoons H_2CO_3(aq) \rightleftharpoons H^+(aq) + HCO_3^-(aq)$$

a What effect does high $Na^+(aq)$ concentration have on both equilibria?
b Explain what effect the presence of $NH_3(aq)$ has on both equilibria.
c Explain the effect of increasing the pressure of $CO_2(g)$.
d If the brine was very dilute what would be the effect on the yield?
e The final precipitation reaction is exothermic and requires cooling. What would be the effect of a breakdown in the cooling arrangements?

2 Write equations for and name the products in the following reactions which occur in the manufacture of sodium carbonate.
a heating of limestone
b heating a mixture of ammonium chloride and quicklime
c heating sodium hydrogen carbonate

Explain, using the equations
d why the process is very economical
e why, once the initial amount of ammonia has been added, no additional ammonia is needed.

18.2   Manufacture of sodium hydroxide and chlorine

1 a Draw a diagram to illustrate the commercial electrolysis of brine.
b Describe the composition of anode and cathode, name the products released at these electrodes and write ionic equations for the reactions taking place.
c Explain fully why it is necessary for one electrode to be a flowing liquid.
d What must be done to liberate sodium hydroxide and then concentrate it to form solid pellets?
e Electrolytic processes are expensive. What makes this process economically viable?

2 Brine may be electrolysed very simply using carbon electrodes (see diagram).

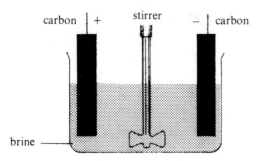

a What will be the product of reactions at (i) anode, (ii) cathode? Write ionic equations.

b If the solution is stirred vigorously during electrolysis the anode and cathode products will mix. What products will be formed? Write an equation.

c The product from **b** is a bleach. Write an equation to represent the reaction which takes place when it bleaches.

d When the product from **c** is heated a gas which relights a glowing splint is produced. Write an equation for this reaction.

3 Sodium hydroxide will react with many chemicals. Write equations and indicate how it reacts with the following:

a ammonium sulphate(VI)   d sulphuric(IV) acid
b aluminium   e iron(II) sulphate(VI)
c phosphorus

18.3 Hydrogen chloride and chlorine

1 a Describe how hydrogen chloride is manufactured industrially.

b Describe how hydrogen chloride is prepared in the laboratory. Write an equation for the reaction.

c Hydrogen chloride is a dipolar, covalent gas. Explain what this means.

d How would you show that dilute hydrochloric acid contains chloride ions?

2 Explain the following observations and write equations where they are appropriate.

a When NaCl is heated with $MnO_2(s)$ and concentrated sulphuric(VI) acid a green gas is given off.

b The green gas bubbled into litmus solution turns it colourless.

c When the green gas is passed over heated steel wool in a combustion tube a red glow appears and brown fumes are produced which sublime to a black solid on the cooler parts of the tube.

d When the green gas is bubbled into colourless potassium iodide solution it first turns brown then deposits a black solid.

e When the green gas is bubbled into water saturated with $H_2S(g)$ a yellow-white deposit is obtained.

18.4 Manufacture of soap

a Describe briefly the commercial preparation of soap.
b How does soap soften hard water?
c How does soap work to remove dirt and grease?
d In what two ways does the function of soap in **b** interfere with its function in **c**?
e Why are detergents more effective than soap for most washing purposes?

18.5 Manufacture of sodium

Two methods may be used to prepare sodium. Nowadays one is not viable although it was the original method used by Davy, the discoverer of sodium.

method A	method B
electrolysis of $NaCl/CaCl_2$ mixture at 900 K	electrolysis of NaOH at 400 K

a Write ionic equations for the reactions taking place at anode and cathode in each case.
b In one case very careful segregation of anode and cathode products was necessary because of the danger of explosion. Why might this occur?
c In one process steam is spontaneously given off causing certain problems. Describe these problems.
d What might be the relative economic advantages and disadvantages of the two methods? (Ignore technical difficulties.)

Objective test 18

Questions 1–8   Apply Rubric A instructions

1 Which of the following **cannot** be made *directly* by the electrolysis of brine?

A chlorine
B sodium hydroxide
C hydrogen

D hydrogen chloride
E sodium chlorate(I)

2 Which of the following is **not** a property of sodium carbonate?
A It gives CO_2 with acid.
B It crystallises with $10H_2O$ in the formula.
C It is alkaline to litmus.
D It gives a golden glow to a bunsen flame.
E It gives off CO_2 when heated.

3 Which of the following statements is **untrue** if applied to caustic soda?
A It is an alkaline solid.
B It decomposes on heating to oxide and water.
C It is a basic hydroxide.
D It can be made by the action of sodium on water.
E It has a soapy feel.

4 Which of the following is **not** true of chlorine?
A It is a poisonous gas.
B When bubbled into water it gives oxygen.
C It bleaches damp litmus.
D It liberates iodine when bubbled into KI(aq).
E It burns in hydrogen giving hydrogen chloride.

5 Which of the following solids will **not** be formed by passing dry chlorine gas over the heated metal?
A $FeCl_2$ B $AlCl_3$ C $ZnCl_2$ D PCl_3 E NaCl

6 When dry hydrogen chloride gas is passed over heated iron, which does **not** apply?
A It glows red.
B It reacts to give glistening black crystals.
C Hydrogen is formed.
D Iron(III) chloride is formed.
E A gas which sublimes is formed.

7 Which statement does **not** apply to hydrogen chloride?
A It is a colourless gas.
B It is an anhydride of hydrochloric acid.
C It reacts with ammonia giving dense white fumes.
D It fumes in moist air.
E It decomposes to hydrogen and chlorine when warmed.

8 Which of the following is **not** true of sodium?
A It dissolves in alcohol giving hydrogen.
B It reduces aluminium oxide to aluminium.
C It is denser than molten sodium chloride.
D It dissolves in mercury.
E It forms more than one oxide.

The following chemicals are involved in the Solvay process.

A $CaCl_2$ B $NaHCO_3$ C CaO D NH_4Cl E $CaCO_3$

9 Which chemical is a product with little usefulness?

10 Which two chemicals heated together give ammonia?

11 Which two chemicals give carbon dioxide when heated?

12 Which chemical is a fairly cheap, quarried material?

13 Which two chemicals contain the ions from which the final product derives?

Sodium carbonate is used

A as a water softener   D for making caustic soda
B in soap making   E for making basic carbonates.
C for making glass

Choose A–E to apply to the following equations

14 $Ca^{2+}(aq) + Na_2CO_3 \longrightarrow CaCO_3(s) + 2Na^+(aq)$

15 $2C_nH_{2n}COOGl + Na_2CO_3 + H_2O \longrightarrow$
$$2C_nH_{2n}COONa + 2GlOH + CO_2$$

16 $Ca(OH)_2 + Na_2CO_3 \longrightarrow 2NaOH + CaCO_3$

17 $SiO_2 + Na_2CO_3 \longrightarrow Na_2SiO_3 + CO_2$

18 $3ZnSO_4 + 5Na_2CO_3 + 6H_2O \longrightarrow$
$$ZnCO_3\,2Zn(OH)_2\,2H_2O + 4NaHCO_3 + 3Na_2SO_4$$

Chlorides may be

A acidic   D oxidising agents
B neutral   E reducing agents.
C insoluble

Choose A–E to apply to the following. More than one letter may apply.

19 carbon tetrachloride

20 phosphorus pentachloride

21 potassium chloride

22 aluminium chloride

23 hydrogen chloride

24 silver(I) chloride

25 Which of the following chemicals are essential in the ammonia-soda process?
  1 brine   2 calcium carbonate   3 ammonia chloride
  4 carbon dioxide

26 Which of the following are adequate explanations of the alkalinity of Na_2CO_3?
  1 It reacts with water forming sodium ions and hydroxide ions.
  2 It is the salt of a weak acid and a strong base.
  3 The carbonate ion reacts with water to form hydrogen carbonate and hydroxide ions.
  4 The carbonate ion reacts with water to form hydroxide ions and carbon dioxide.

27 In which of the following is HCl oxidised?
  1 $AgNO_3 + HCl \longrightarrow AgCl + HNO_3$
  2 $MnO_4^- (aq) + 8HCl \longrightarrow MnCl_2 + 4H_2O + 3Cl_2$
  3 $NH_3 + HCl \longrightarrow NH_4Cl$
  4 $PbO_2 + 4HCl \longrightarrow PbCl_2 + 2H_2O + Cl_2$

28 Which of the following is true of the Downs process for making sodium?
  1 $CaCl_2$ is added to lower the mp of NaCl.
  2 The chlorine and sodium must be segregated carefully.
  3 Sodium is separated because it is immiscible with molten NaCl.
  4 Sodium is given off at the carbon anode.

29 Chlorine may be used commercially
  1 directly as a bleach
  2 to make sodium chloride
  3 to purify water
  4 to fumigate greenhouses.

30 Which of the following domestic products derive, in part, from brine?
  1 Domestos   2 Tide   3 baking powder   4 Epsom salts

Chapter 19   Limestone

1 Identify A, B, C, D and E.

A was a white solid. After prolonged heating it crumbled to a white powder, B. The cooled, white powder reacted violently with water producing steam and a white slurry, C. When C was filtered a colourless liquid, D, was the filtrate. D turned milky when carbon dioxide was passed into it. Further amounts of carbon dioxide produced the colourless solution, E.

Write equations for all the reactions taking place.

2 The following is a description of how to make soap in the laboratory. Explain the procedures underlined.

5 cm³ of castor oil was placed in a conical flask and a solution containing 10 g of NaOH in 20 cm³ of water was added. The mixture was boiled and thoroughly agitated for 5–10 minutes. 5 g of ordinary salt was added and the mixture allowed to cool. The precipitate was filtered off and then washed with successive small quantities of water. The residue was pressed between sheets of filter paper. Then the residue was dissolved in the minimum quantity of hot alcohol. On cooling fine white crystals of soap formed. They were filtered off and left above a radiator.

3 Explain the reasons for the following:

    a Many farmers spread large quantities of ground limestone onto their fields in the late autumn.

    b An important rule of gardening is never to add both fresh manure and hydrated lime to the soil at the same time.

    c If a soil contains a lot of clay then it is recommended that lime be added to it.

    d In metal smelting, limestone is almost invariably added to the molten impure metal.

    e Hydrated lime is added to sand to make mortar.

Objective test 19

Questions 1–4   Apply Rubric A instructions

1 Which of the following is a metamorphic form of limestone?
   A calcite   B limestone rock   C marble   D stalactites   E chalk

2 Which of the following is true of water in both hard and soft water areas?
   A always contains HCO_3^- ions
   B always contains Ca^{2+} ions
   C always contains $CaCO_3$ molecules
   D always contains $Ca(HCO_3)_2$ molecules
   E always contains $CaSO_4$ molecules

3 Which of the following is the hardest water?
   A well water   B rain water   C sea water   D distilled water
   E river water

4 Which of the following reactions represents the formation of a stalactite?
   A $Ca(HCO_3)_2 \longrightarrow CaCO_3 + H_2O + CO_2$
   B $Ca(OH)_2 + 2CO_2 \longrightarrow Ca(HCO_3)_2$
   C $CaCO_3 + H_2O + CO_2 \longrightarrow Ca(HCO_3)_2$
   D $Ca(OH)_2 + CO_2 \longrightarrow CaCO_3 + H_2O$
   E $Ca(HCO_3)_2 \longrightarrow Ca(OH)_2 + 2CO_2$

Questions 5–11   Apply Rubric B instructions

Indicate which of the following A–E apply to the descriptions below.
   A $CaSO_4$ B $Ca(HCO_3)_2$ C $Ca(OH)_2$ D $CaCl_2$ E $CaCO_3$

5 Formed when slaked lime is left exposed to the air (as in mortar).

6 Incorporated in school chalk.

7 Starting material for stalagmites.

8 Very soluble in water making it permanently hard.

9 Effervesce when acid is added.

10 Their solutions turn milky with carbon dioxide.

11 Soluble in water making it temporarily hard.

12 Which of the following apply to soap?
   1 It does not produce a scum with hard water.
   2 It softens hard water quickly and effectively.
   3 It is cheaper to use with hard water than other chemicals.
   4 It is kind to the complexion.

13 Which of the following are true of detergents (**not** washing powders)?
   1 They cause a lather so making grease and dirt float.
   2 They attach to particles of grease and dislodge them.
   3 They make the water soft by precipitating all the calcium salts.
   4 They are long chain molecules with salt-like properties at one end
     and covalent-like properties at the other end.

14 Which of the following are advantages of hard water?
   1 It provides for healthy teeth.
   2 It builds up scale in lead pipes preventing poisonous lead salts
     from entering the water.
   3 It makes the water taste better.
   4 It prevents the lathering of soap.

15 Which of the following methods will only **partly** soften hard water?
   1 adding washing soda
   2 adding detergent
   3 adding sodium aluminium silicate
   4 boiling it

	assertion		*reason*
16	A high temperature is used to make quicklime.	*because*	The reaction is exothermic.
17	Energy (heat) is given out when quicklime dissolves.	*because*	Ionic solids always dissolve giving out heat.
18	The equilibrium $CaCO_3 \rightleftharpoons CaO + CO_2$ moves to the right when the CO_2 concentration is lowered.	*because*	The rate of the back reaction is dependent on CO_2 concentration.
19	Calcium carbonate is more stable than sodium carbonate to heat.	*because*	Calcium is divalent but sodium is only monovalent.

Chapter 20 Extraction of metals

1 Answer the following, which refer to the electrolytic methods of preparing sodium and aluminium.

    a Why is molten aluminium tapped off the bottom of the cell but sodium is tapped off the top?

    b What is the purpose of the cryolite added in the production of aluminium?

    c Why is the consumption of electricity larger for aluminium production?

    d The carbon anodes in aluminium production have to be continually replaced. Why is this?

    e Write ionic equations for the anode and cathode reactions taking place in the electrolytic manufacture of sodium and aluminium.

2 Answer the following, which refer to iron production.

    a What is the purpose of lining the steel furnace with fire-brick?

    b Why is the air blown in pre-heated to $800°C$?

    c What is the purpose of adding limestone?

    d At what temperature does the iron melt (approximately)?

    e At what temperature does the iron(III) oxide get reduced and by what chemical?

Write equations for the principal reactions which take place in the blast furnace.

3 There are basically five stages in the preparation of a metal from its ore.

    a crushing

    b separation and enrichment of ore particles

    c roasting of the ore in air

    d reduction of the ore with carbon

    e purification of the crude metal

Explain how each stage is carried out by reference to the preparation of zinc.

Objective test 20

Question 1 & 2   Apply Rubric A instructions

1 Which of the following impurities is **not** likely to be present in pig iron?

    A carbon   B phosphorus   C silica   D sulphur   E chromium

2 Which of the following is most suitable for extracting sulphur in molten metal?

    A silica   B oxygen   C limestone   D carbon   E the metal oxide

Questions 3–11   Apply Rubric B instructions

Choose from the list A–E those metals which apply to the statements following.

    A K   B Hg   C Al   D Au   E Zn

3 Extracted by electrolysis of the chloride.

4 Extracted from its oxide by heating only.

5 Extracted by electrolysis of the fused oxide.

6 Made from its oxide by reduction with CO.

7 Highest in the electrochemical series.

8 Lowest in the electrochemical series.

9 Found native.

10 Tarnish rapidly in air.

11 Protected by thin layer of oxide.

Questions 12 & 13   Apply Rubric C instructions

12 Which of the following is true of the open hearth and Bessemer processes?

    1 The furnace lining is basic and absorbs acid impurities.
    2 The temperature must be high enough to keep the iron molten.
    3 The carbon content is carefully adjusted to the ideal level.
    4 The oxidation of impurities is brought about by haematite.

13 Which of the following is true of wrought iron?

    1 It is the purest form of iron.
    2 It is very brittle at room temperature.
    3 It can be wrought into fancy shapes at high temperature.
    4 It is used as a structural material in buildings.

assertion		reason
14 The element rubidium is made by the electrolysis of fused chloride.	*because*	It is high in the electrochemical series and cannot be reduced with carbon.
15 Oxygen is blown through the Bessemer converter.	*because*	Impurities are oxidised and escape as gases.
16 Iron rusts very quickly in the desert.	*because*	High temperature increases reaction rates.
17 Zinc is not used for cooking utensils.	*because*	Zinc salts are poisonous.
18 Aluminium is used for high tension electric cables.	*because*	It conducts better than copper.
19 Copper may be made by allowing copper(II) sulphate (VI) to percolate over scrap iron.	*because*	Iron is lower in the reactivity series than copper.

Chapter 21   The chemistry of metals

1 Explain the following observations with regard to metal salts.
a Aluminium chloride fumed in moist air and dissolved violently in water giving off a gas which produced white fumes with ammonia.
b Sodium nitrate(V) melted when heated. On fierce heating it effervesced and a gas which relighted a glowing splint was given off. The cooled residue decolourised purple potassium manganate(VII).
c Sodium hydroxide reacted with aluminium vigorously, giving off a gas which burned with a 'pop'. When water was added to the clear solution, a white precipitate resulted.
d Lead(II) nitrate(V) crackled when heated and gave off a brown gas which seemed to relight a glowing splint. The yellow material left fused with the glass and caused it to crack.
e When H_2S gas was bubbled into an acidified solution of zinc(II) sulphate(VI) nothing happened. When the solution was neutralised with ammonia a white precipitate of zinc sulphide formed.

2 Explain how you would distinguish between the following (i) physically (ii) chemically.
a iron(II) chloride solution and iron(III) chloride solution
b copper(I) oxide and copper(II) oxide
c lead(IV) oxide and red lead
d sodium chloride solution and potassium chloride solution
e sodium sulphate(VI) solution and sodium sulphate(IV) solution

3 Explain the following:
a Copper is used instead of lead in modern plumbing.
b Copper pipes should not come directly in contact with steel radiators.
c Aluminium windows are better than steel framed windows.
d Galvanised sheets are usually corrugated.
e Copper vessels should not be used to store wines.
f Lead roofs 'creep'.
g Copper roofs go green.
h Steel rods are inserted in concrete for pillars but not in concrete for ground floors.
i Sodium is used as a coolant in a fast breeder reactor.

4 Identify the compounds A–E and write equations for the reactions involved.
A green substance, A, was heated gently. A black substance, B, resulted. B was reacted with dilute nitric(V) acid and dissolved to give a blue solution, C. C was evaporated to a small volume in a fume cupboard when blue-green crystals, D, separated. The crystals were filtered off and transferred to an ignition tube. On heating brown fumes were given off and a black material, identical with B, formed. When the original substance, A, was added to HCl there was a vigorous effervescence and a green solution, E, was formed.

Objective test 21

Questions 1–6   Apply Rubric B instructions

Choose from A–E the right answer(s) to questions 1–6.
A carbonate   D hydrogen carbonate
B oxide   E chloride
C sulphate(VI)

1 React with an acid with effervescence.

2 Dissolves in water giving an alkaline solution.

3 Decomposes when heated giving off steam and carbon dioxide.

4 Give white precipitate with silver ion solutions.

5 An acidified solution gives a white precipitate with barium solutions.

6 Heating with concentrated sulphuric(VI) acid gives a gas which fumes in moist air.

Questions 7–10   Apply Rubric C instructions

7 Which of the following are metals?
   1 mp 98°C, conducts, density 0·97, soft, reacts with water
   2 mp 114°C, non-conductor, density 4·94, brittle, insoluble in water and dil. HCl
   3 mp 1083°C, conductor, density 8·92, malleable, insoluble in water and dil. HCl
   4 mp 3000 + °C, conductor, density 2·25, brittle, insoluble in water and dil. HCl

8 Which is true of hydrated iron(II) sulphate(VI)?
   1 It contains seven mol water of crystallisation per mol of salt.
   2 It decomposes when heated to iron(II) sulphate(IV).
   3 It is used in the brown ring test for nitrates(V).
   4 It is made by adding dilute sulphuric(VI) acid to iron(II) chloride.

9 Which is true of transition elements?
   1 They are all metals.
   2 The elements all form coloured hydrates.
   3 The elements exhibit many valencies.
   4 The elements have two electrons in their outer electron shell.

10 Which is/are acceptable methods of making iron(III) chloride?
   1 Passing dry HCl(g) over heated iron.
   2 Dissolving iron in dilute HCl(aq) and evaporating to dryness.
   3 Passing dry HCl(g) over iron(III) oxide.
   4 Passing dry Cl_2(g) over heated iron.

	assertion		reason

11 Aluminium is used in cables for power transmission.   *because*   It is a better conductor than copper weight for weight.

12 Sodium boils at a lower temperature than magnesium.   *because*   Sodium has a lower ionisation energy than magnesium.

13 Noble metals displace hydrogen from dilute hydrochloric acid.   *because*   They are lower than hydrogen in the electrochemical series.

14 A flame test can be used to detect many metals.   *because*   Their outer electrons are able to absorb light energy.

15 Iron(III) chloride is acidic.   *because*   It gives off $HCl(g)$ which dissolves in water.

16 Zinc(II) chloride is used as a flux in soldering.   *because*   It forms a bond between the solder and the metal to be soldered.

17 Lead forms three oxides.   *because*   It is a variable valency transition element.

18 Potassium carbonate gives carbon dioxide when heated.   *because*   It is unstable at high temperatures.

19 Salt accelerates the precipitation of mud from muddy water.   *because*   It neutralises the small charged particles of fine mud.

20 Metals increase in density when heated.   *because*   The metal atoms occupy more space when the metal is hot.

Chapter 22   Sulphur and its compounds

22.1   Extraction

The following questions relate to the Frasch process represented by the three concentric pipes in the diagram.

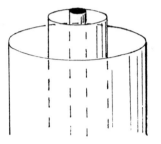

a What flows down the inner pipe?
b What flows down the outer pipe?
c What flows up the pipe in between?
d To what depth are the pipes usually lowered?
e Explain why it is possible to obtain sulphur of over 99% purity.
f What advantages does this process have over mining sulphur from sulphur-bearing rocks?

22.2   Allotropes

The following are instructions for preparing monoclinic sulphur. Explain the items underlined.

Add small quantities of crushed roll sulphur to a flask containing 20 cm^3 of xylene. Fit a reflux condenser to the flask and boil the xylene gently. Keep adding sulphur down the condenser until no more will dissolve. Cool the solution slowly. When needle-like crystals have formed decant off the xylene. Place the crystals between sheets of filter paper.

Why is xylene used to make monoclinic sulphur but carbon disulphide used to make rhombic sulphur? The manipulations and method are the same for both.

22.3 Sulphur dioxide

Explain the following:

   a The concentration of sulphur dioxide in the atmosphere can be estimated by studying lichen growth.

   b Recently it was stated that sulphur dioxide concentrations had fallen so much that the black spot disease of sycamore leaves was reappearing.

   c The concentration of sulphur dioxide in the air is increased when an atmospheric 'inversion' takes place.

   d Norway suffers from rivers with a high acidity which discourages fish growth.

   e Organic material decaying underwater often smells of rotten eggs.

22.4 Conversion of sulphur dioxide to sulphur(VI) oxide

1 Large quantities of sulphuric(VI) acid are used to make the fertiliser, ammonium sulphate(VI).

   a How many kg of concentrated sulphuric(VI) acid are required to make 1 kg of ammonium sulphate?

   b Assuming that 1 kg is sufficient to supply nitrogen to the surface soil, 10 cm deep, over an area of 10 m^2, what would be the concentration of ammonium sulphate(VI) in g dm^{-3}?

   c What would be the concentration of nitrogen in the same units?

   d Assuming that all the sulphate(VI) is converted back to sulphuric(VI) acid, making the ground acidic, what amount of calcium carbonate would have to be spread over the same ground to neutralise this?

2 Explain the following:

   a SO$_3$ gas is dissolved in concentrated sulphuric(VI) acid and not water.

   b Concentrated sulphuric(VI) acid is made by adding water to 'oleum'.

   c A solution of sulphuric(IV) acid gives a white precipitate with barium chloride solution which disappears when dilute hydrochloric acid is added.

   d When a drop of sulphuric(VI) acid is heated with castor oil the resulting compound gives a lather with water.

   e Concentrated sulphuric(VI) acid added to water is far less dangerous than water added to concentrated sulphuric(VI) acid.

22.5 Hydrogen sulphide

1 indicate what you see   **2** write equations for
the reaction of hydrogen sulphide gas with the following solutions:

   a zinc(II) sulphate(VI) solution

   b copper(II) sulphate(VI) solution

   c lead(II) nitrate(V) solution

   d sulphuric(VI) acid solution

   e chlorine water

In which of the above is hydrogen sulphide reacting as a reducing agent?

Objective test 22

Questions 1–5   Apply Rubric A instructions

1 Which of the following contains 9·8 g of sulphuric(VI) acid?
A 10 cm³ 0·1M H_2SO_4 D 1 litre 0·1M H_2SO_4
B 10 cm³ 1M H_2SO_4 E 100 cm³ 0·1M H_2SO_4
C 1 litre 1M H_2SO_4

2 Which of the following volumes of SO_2 at s.t.p. is sufficient to make 1 dm³ of 0·1M sulphuric(VI) acid?
A 22·4 dm³ B 2·24 dm³   C 1·12 dm³ D 11·2 dm³ E 0·224 dm³

3 Which of the following amounts of H_2S can theoretically be obtained from iron(II) sulphide and 1 dm³ of 1M HCl (at s.t.p.)?
A 22·4 dm³   B 11·2 dm³   C 44·8 dm³   D 5·6 dm³   E 2·24 dm³

4 Which of the following is the weakest acid?
A H_2SO_4 B HCl   C H_2S D H_2SO_3 E NH_4Cl

5 Which of the following is the likely molecular formula of sulphur?
A S_2 B S_4 C S   D S_8 E S_6

Questions 6–10   Apply Rubric B instructions

Sulphuric(VI) acid may be
A a dehydrating agent   D hygroscopic
B an oxidant   E a displacer of lower boiling acids from
C an acid   their salts

6 Gives a black mass of carbon with paper.

7 Effervesces with magnesium ribbon giving a gas which burns with a pop.

8 Heated with copper gives sulphur dioxide.

9 Blue copper(II) sulphate(VI) crystals turn white in the acid.

10 Heated with sodium nitrate(V) it produces brown, acidic fumes.

Questions 11–15   Apply Rubric C instructions

11 Which of the following conditions optimise the production of SO_3 from SO_2?
    1 vanadium(V) pentoxide catalyst
    2 excess of SO_2
    3 temperature of 450°C
    4 low pressure

12 Which of the following are **conclusive** test(s) for SO_2?
  1 It decolourises bromine water.
  2 It turns starch-iodate paper blue.
  3 It turns dark brown iodine solution colourless.
  4 It turns potassium dichromate(IV) paper emerald green.

13 Which of the following apply to $SO_3(g)$?
  1 It is easily liquefied.
  2 It does not dissolve easily in water.
  3 It is a strong oxidising agent.
  4 It supports the burning of a lighted splint.

14 Which of the following apply to hydrogen sulphide?
  1 It burns with a blue flame.
  2 It is produced as a result of aerobic decomposition.
  3 It is very poisonous—more so than hydrogen cyanide.
  4 It is very soluble in water.

15 Which of the following processes need sulphuric(VI) acid?
  1 detergent manufacture
  2 the lime-soda process
  3 making explosives like TNT
  4 fermentation

Questions 16–19   Apply Rubric D instructions

	assertion		*reason*
16	Concentrated sulphuric (VI) acid does not act as an acid.	*because*	Concentrated sulphuric(VI) acid is a covalent substance.
17	Anhydrite is used to prepare sulphuric(VI) acid.	*because*	It gives off $SO_3(g)$ when it is heated strongly.
18	Sulphur candles were burned in old barrels.	*because*	Sulphur dioxide is an effective fumigant.
19	Ammonium sulphate(VI) is acidic.	*because*	The sulphate(VI) ion reacts with water to give an acid.

Answers to objective tests

Objective test 1

1 C   2 C   3 E   4 D   5 D   6 D   7 A   8 A

Objective test 2

1 D   2 D   3 E   4 C   5 E   6 D   7 B   8 C

Objective test 3

1 C   2 B   3 C   4 C   5 B   6 A

Objective test 4

1 B   2 C   3 C   4 A   5 D   6 E   7 D   8 C   9 B   10 C

Objective test 5

1 C   2 D   3 D   4 B   5 E

Objective test 6

1 E   2 D   3 E   4 D   5 B   6 A   7 D   8 C   9 A   10 A
11 C   12 E

Objective test 7

1 C   2 E   3 C   4 A   5 A   6 E   7 D   8 B   9 C   10 A

Objective test 8

1 A   2 E   3 D   4 D   5 B   6 D   7 E   8 C   9 A

Objective test 9

1 C   2 C   3 E   4 A   5 B   6 C   7 D   8 E

Objective test 10

1 B   2 C   3 B   4 C   5 E   6 E   7 A   8 E   9 A   10 E   11 B
12 D   13 C   14 C   15 A   16 E   17 B   18 D   19 C   20 A
21 E   22 D   23 B   24 A   25 B

Objective test 11

1 B   2 C   3 E   4 B   5 C   6 C   7 A   8 D   9 B   10 E   11 E
12 A & D   13 A & B   14 C   15 D   16 D   17 B   18 A   19 D
20 A

Objective test 12

1 E   2 E   3 C   4 B & C   5 A   6 A, B & D   7 E   8 A   9 A
10 C

Objective test 13

1 D   2 C   3 C   4 E   5 A   6 D   7 B   8 B & C   9 E   10 E
11 C   12 B   13 D   14 A   15 B   16 A & E   17 B & D   18 C
19 B   20 C   21 C   22 A   23 D   24 E   25 A & E   26 B & C
27 E   28 A, D & E   29 D   30 E   31 C   32 A   33 B   34 B
35 B   36 C   37 A

Objective test 14

1 B   2 C   3 E   4 C   5 C   6 B   7 A   8 E   9 D   10 B   11 C
12 A   13 E   14 D   15 B   16 A   17 C   18 A

Objective test 15

1 C   2 E   3 A   4 E   5 C   6 E   7 D   8 A & C   9 D   10 E
11 C   12 B   13 A   14 E   15 D   16 C   17 A   18 A   19 B

Objective test 16

1 A   2 A   3 E   4 C   5 C   6 D   7 B   8 A   9 E   10 A & D
11 B & C   12 A, D & E   13 B   14 C   15 D   16 B   17 A

Objective test 17

1 C   2 B   3 D   4 E   5 A   6 B   7 C   8 D   9 F   10 E   11 C
12 B

Objective test 18

1 D   2 E   3 B   4 B   5 A   6 D   7 E   8 C   9 A   10 C & D
11 B & E   12 E   13 B & E   14 A   15 B   16 D   17 C   18 E
19 B & C   20 A & D   21 B   22 A   23 A & E   24 B & C   25 A
26 A   27 C   28 A   29 B   30 A

Objective test 19

1 C   2 A   3 C   4 A   5 E   6 A   7 B   8 D   9 B & E   10 C & D
11 B   12 C   13 C   14 A   15 D   16 C   17 C   18 A   19 D

Objective test 20

1 E   2 B   3 A   4 B   5 C   6 E   7 A   8 D   9 D   10 A, C & E
11 C   12 A   13 B   14 A   15 A   16 D   17 A   18 C   19 C

Objective test 21

1 A & D   2 B   3 D   4 A, D & E   5 C   6 E   7 B   8 B   9 B
10 D   11 A   12 B   13 D   14 C   15 A   16 C   17 C   18 E
19 A   20 D

Objective test 22

1 D   2 B   3 B   4 C   5 D   6 A   7 C   8 B   9 D   10 E   11 B
12 D   13 A   14 B   15 B   16 A   17 C   18 A   19 C

General answers

Chapter 2

2.2 1 a A & D **b** A, B, C, F & G **c** D & E **f** F
g 286 kJ mol^{-1}

2.4 1 NO **2** water **3** Mn **4** hydrogen gas

Chapter 3

3.1 2 a 0·00001 g **b** 0·00000001 g **c** less than 10^{-8} g
d 16 times **3 a** 0·0004 g **b** 0·00004 g **c** 0·00004 g
d 100d cm^3 **e** 0·0000004 cm **4** volume, 3 × 10^{-23} cm^3;
diameter, between 10^{-7} and 10^{-8}

3.2 1 c propane; 11/7

3.4 1 a 20 cm^3 CO$_2$ **b** 5 cm^3 C$_3$H$_8$; 25 cm^3 oxygen
c 2 dm^3 hydrogen **2 a** 100 cm^3 **b** 1 volume 3 volumes
2 volumes **c** A + 3B ⟶ 2C **3** 880 cm^3; − 10°C; 1140 mm

Chapter 5

5.2 2 a 24, 26 **b** 24, 26 **c** 12 **d** isotopes **e** 24·2

Chapter 6

6.3 2 SCl$_2$ 2; SF$_6$ 6; CO$_2$ 4; P$_2$O$_3$ 6; C$_2$H$_6$ 7 **3** greatest, CO$_2$;
smallest, H$_2$O **5 a** C **b** B & D **c** A & D or A & B
d E & D **e** B & D

Chapter 8

8.1 2 a 56 **b** 95 **c** 188 **d** 342

8.2 1 a 10 pannards **b** 2$\frac{1}{2}$ pannards; type of brick **c** 17 600 kg
d yes **2 a** 10 mol; 320 g **b** 2 mol **c** 240 g **d** yes
e 48·16 × 10^{23}; 36·12 × 10^{23} **3 a** 246 **b** 246:24 **c** 2·46 g
d 0·01 mol **e** 0·01 mol **4 a** 0·16 g **b** 0·01 mol **c** 0·02 mol
d 2:1 **e** Cu$_2$O

8.3 b 1:1 **c** 0·01 mol **d** 1·435 g **e** 0·585 g

8.4 b 0·0025 mol **c** 0·0050 mol **d** 100 cm^3 **e** 0·0355 g

8.5 1 a 1000 m^3 **b** 4000 m^3 **c** 1000 m^3 **d** 0·8035 kg **e** 2·4105 kg
2 b $\dfrac{0·03}{A}$ mol **c** $\dfrac{3}{2240}$ **d** 22·4 **e** $\dfrac{300}{273}$ **3 b** 0·05 mol
c 0·04 mol **d** 0·02 mol **e** 2 g; 88·88%

Chapter 9

9.1 **a** 9 g **b** 4 g **c** 5 g **d** 10 g 5 g

9.3 **1** 396 kJ mol^{-1} **2** 312 kJ mol^{-1}

9.4 **1 b** 1 mol **c** 1 mol **d** 22·4 dm^3 at s.t.p. **e** 243 kJ mol^{-1}
f 243 kJ mol^{-1} **g** less **2 a** CH_4(methane) **c** CH_4
3 a 750 J **b** 22 500 J **c** 40 500 J mol^{-1} **d** 9750 J; 117 000 J
4 a 16·8 kJ mol^{-1} **b** kJ mol^{-1} **5 a** 2·919 kJ **b** 0·05 mol
c 58·38 kJ mol^{-1}

Chapter 10

10.2 **2 a** high temperature **b** no

10.3 **c** 160 cm^3 **d** reaction complete at 224 cm^3 of CO_2 **e** 1 g

Chapter 11

11.2 **1 d** 0·01 mol H_2, 0·005 mol O_2; 224 cm^3 H_2, 112 cm^3 O_2
e 965 seconds **2 c** 112 dm^3 **d** 0·1 g **e** 4 F (Faradays)

11.3 **a** 108 g **b** 0·01 F **c** 0·1 amp (approx) **d** 0·32 g **e** 2

Chapter 12

4 a A **c** E **d** E

Chapter 13

13.1 **3 d** 448 cm^3 N_2(g) s.t.p. **e** 0·0045 g

13.2 **1 a** (ii)

13.4 **2 a** 15 vol **b** $\frac{1}{2}$ mol **c** $\frac{3}{224}$ (0·0134) mol **d** 1·34 M **e** 1·79 M

Chapter 14

14.3 **2 a** 1·26 g **b** 126 g **c** MSO_4 7H_2O; atomic mass 24
d molecular mass

Chapter 19

1 A is $CaCO_3$; B is CaO; C is $Ca(OH)_2$; D is lime-water;
E is calcium hydrogen carbonate solution

Chapter 21

4 A is $CuCO_3$; B is CuO; C is $Cu(NO_3)_2$(aq); D is
$Cu(NO_3)_2 3H_2O$(c); E is $CuCl_2$(aq)

Chapter 22

22.4 **1** **a** 0.7656 kg   **b** 0.07656 g dm^{-3}
c 0.01675 g dm^{-3} **d** 0.7813 kg